A RE-INTI

THOMA.   ᴧʀY

VOLᴜME 2

A Re-Introduction
to
Thomas Newberry
VOLUME 2

THE EXPECTED ONE

THE PERFECTIONS
AND EXCELLENCIES OF
HOLY SCRIPTURE

JOHN RITCHIE LTD
CHRISTIAN PUBLICATIONS

40 Beansburn, Kilmarnock, Scotland

ISBN-13: 978 1 904064 88 6
ISBN-10: 1 904064 88 4

Copyright © 2009 by John Ritchie Ltd.
40 Beansburn, Kilmarnock, Scotland

www.ritchiechristianmedia.co.uk

The *Classic Reprint Series* is derived from facsimile copies of the originally published material.

At times the quality of print and typeface may have been compromised as a result of either inferior original copy or the facsimile process itself.

We are confident, however, that the vast majority of the printed content is of reasonable quality and most importantly is legible.

Typeset by John Ritchie Ltd., Kilmarnock
Printed by Bell & Bain Ltd., Glasgow

THE EXPECTED ONE

The
Expected One

or

The Coming of the Son of God from Heaven

and

His Manifestation as Son of Man to Earth

Contents.

——:o:——

THE PENTECOSTAL CHURCH, ... 5

THE COMING OF THE SON OF GOD, ... 15

THE JUDGMENT SEAT OF CHRIST, ... 19

THE PRESENTATION OF THE RISEN SAINTS, ... 23

THE COMING OF OUR LORD JESUS CHRIST, ... 27

THE TIMES AND SEASONS, ... 33

THE MANIFESTATION OF THE LORD IN FLAMING FIRE, ... 38

THE APOSTASY, ... 42

THE REVELATION OF THE MAN OF SIN,... 46

THE WITHHOLDER, ... 50

THE FALSE PROPHET, ... 54

THE OUTWARD CHARACTERISTICS OF THIS DISPENSATION, 58

THE LAST WEEK OF DANIEL'S SEVENTY WEEKS OF YEARS, 64

PARABLE OF THE FIG TREE AND THE DAYS OF NOAH, ... 69

PARABLES OF THE HOUSEHOLDER AND THE SERVANTS, ... 75

PARABLE OF THE TEN VIRGINS, ... 82

PARABLE OF THE TALENTS, ... 87

THE JUDGMENT OF THE LIVING NATIONS, ... 94

THE PENTECOSTAL CHURCH.

————)≍(————

WE must carefully distinguish between Israel,
as the wife of Jehovah, the subject of Old
Testament prophecy, and the Bride as the Lamb's
wife according to the book of Revelation. Israel
was espoused to Jehovah in the wilderness (Jer. ii.
2), and brought into covenant relationship with God
at Mount Sinai (Jer. xxxi. 31,32). Israel, through sin
and unfaithfulness, put herself away, for it was not
an act of God in fickleness towards her; Jehovah
hateth putting away. "Thus saith Jehovah, where
is the bill of your mother's divorcement, whom I
put away? Or which of My creditors is it to whom
I have sold you? Behold, for your iniquities have
ye sold yourselves, and for your transgressions is
your mother put away." (Isa. l. 1).

It was her own doing. This is the present condition of Israel, as a woman divorced, put away; and

instead of being the people of God, "Ammi," are receiving the title of "Lo-ammi," "not My people," and of "Lo-ruhamah," that is "not having obtained mercy." (Hosea i. 6-9).

Nevertheless God has promised to return to her in time to come, and receive her back into favour. (Hosea i. 10, 11 ; ii. 14-23). Not according to LAW, but according to grace (Jer iii. 1). "They say, If a man put away his wife, and she go from him, and become another man's, shall he return unto her again ? Shall not that land be greatly polluted ? But thou hast played the harlot with many lovers ; yet return again to Me, saith Jehovah ! See also Deut. xxiv. 1-4. He will make a new covenant of GRACE with them, "Behold, the days come, saith Jehovah, that I will make a new covenant with the house of Israel, and with the house of Judah ; not according to the covenant that I made with their fathers in the day that I took them by the hand to bring them out of the land of Egypt; which My covenant they brake, although I was a husband unto them, saith Jehovah. But this shall be the covenant that I will make with the house of Israel. After those days, saith Jehovah, I will put My law in their inward parts, and write it in their hearts, and will be their God, and they shall be My people " (Jer. xxxi. 31-34 ; Heb. viii. 8-12).

Whilst Israel is "Lo-ammi," God has been accomplishing the eternal purpose which He purposed in

Christ Jesus our Lord, that hidden mystery made known to the Apostle Paul (Eph. iii. 1-11). God kept silence concerning this, till the time should come when He would provide a bride for His Son. From the beginning He gave types which shadowed His own intention, purpose and design. For example, He provided for Adam after his deep sleep, a help-meet, Eve.

After Isaac was offered up by Abraham as a type of a crucified and risen Christ, Abraham sent Eliezer to procure a wife for his son. Rebekah as won for Isaac by Eliezer, is a striking illustration of the Church won by the Holy Ghost.

Joseph, rejected by his brethren, sold into Egypt, afterwards set at the right hand of authority and power, had a bride given him in Asenath, to share his glory.

When Moses was rejected by Israel, who he expected would receive him as their deliverer, God provided him a wife in Zipporah.

Solomon exalted to power and splendour, took to wife the King of Egypt's daughter, the bride, the subject of Solomon's Song.

When Naomi was in widowhood—a type of Israel in her desolation, Ruth, the Moabitess, became the wife of Boaz, the mighty man of wealth. All these were designed of God to foreshadow the mystery of the Church, the future Bride, to be presented in due time to Christ, according to Paul's Epistles.

The Beginning of the Church.

The Church, the Bride of the Lamb, commenced with the coming of the Holy Ghost at Pentecost; until then there was no Church on earth.

The expression in Acts vii. 38, "Church in the wilderness," is taken from the Septuagint rendering for "Congregation of Israel." Christ speaks of the Church as a future thing in Matt. xvi. 18, and xviii. 18-20.

Up to Pentecost, there were believing Jews and believing Gentiles. Till Pentecost, they were not baptized into one body; from Pentecost they were baptized by one Spirit into one body, where there is neither Jew nor Gentile, bond nor free, all are one in Christ Jesus (1 Cor. xii. 13; Gal. iii. 27,28). From Pentecost to the return of the Lord Jesus to receive His Church, during the present time, the whole world is divided into three classes—the Jew, the Gentile, and the Church of God.

A Jew or Gentile when born again, receives the Pentecostal Spirit, "But if any man have not the Spirit of Christ, he is none of His" (Rom. viii. 9). When he becomes a believer in Christ he is not regarded as a Jew or a Gentile, but is baptized into the one body where there is neither Jew nor Gentile. This is the peculiarity of the present dispensation: the distinction between Jews and Gentiles ceases, he becomes one of the Church of God, a member of the body of Christ. Now it is the Church dispensation, the dispensation of the Comforter.

This present dispensation comes to a close, when the Spirit of God has accomplished His work as Comforter of regenerating and sanctifying the members of the body of Christ, composed of those given Him in the counsels of eternity by the Father, who are now being cleansed by the washing of water by the word (Eph. v. 26).

We read in John xvii. 2, 6, 9, that the Lord Jesus said to His Father, "Thou hast given Him power over all flesh, that He should give eternal life to as many as Thou hast given Him. I manifested Thy name unto the men which Thou hast given Me out of the world; Thine they were, and Thou hast given them Me. I pray for them: I pray not for the world, but for them which Thou hast given Me, for they are Thine."

The Lord did not then pray for the world, nor for Israel; but like Aaron when he went in with the blood of the bullock into the holiest, it was for himself and his house (Lev. xvi. 6). So Christ in John xvii. asks for glory for Himself as having finished the work, and prays for His house. "Whose house are we" (Heb. iii. 6).

The Church is a gift to Christ out of the election of God. The elect of God are all who believe in Christ from Adam who are "written in the book of life of the Lamb slain, from the foundation of the

world " ‚Rev. xiii. 8). (There is a danger of putting
the comma in the wrong place. There was no Lamb
slain from the foundation of the world, but those
given to Christ were written in the Book of Life
before the foundation of the world). As Eliezer
wooed and won Rebekah for Isaac, as she was given
to him and received to his home ; such is the work
of the Spirit of God now, taking out from among
the Gentiles a people for the Name of God, and a
Bride for the Lamb. When this work is completed,
then we who are alive and remain shall be caught
up together with all who from Abel downward have
died in the faith of Christ, and all who from Stephen
onward have fallen asleep in Jesus, to meet the Lord
in the air on the other side of the clouds (1 Thess. iv.
14-17), and to be for ever with Him. From that
time there is no shadow of intimation of the Church
of God on earth.

During the interval, from "the coming of our
Lord Jesus Christ, and our gathering together unto
Him" (2 Thess. ii. 1), to "the day of Christ" (2
Thess. ii. 2), when He comes with clouds (Rev. i. 7),
there intervenes the last week of Daniel's prophecy
of seventy weeks of years, an interval of at least
seven years. Then Satan will have his synagogue,
Babylon the Great, who subsequently becomes the
habitation of devils, &c. (Rev. xviii. 2). At that
time there will be believing Jews and believing

Gentiles, recognized as such, but not associated together as the church.

At the commencement of the three years and a half, or first half of the week, 144,000 out of all the tribes of the children of Israel will be sealed as servants of God, and recognized as believing Jews (Rev. vii. 2-8); and as the result of the persecution during the latter three and a half years, there will be a multitude which no man can number, out all nations, and kindreds, and people, and tongues, who, having confessed Christ unto death, will stand before the throne of God and the Lamb (Rev. vii. 9, 10). It is an absolute impossibility for the Church of God to be on earth during the times of Antichrist and the great tribulation. In that period, believing Jews are distinctly owned nationally as belonging to the twelve tribes of Israel; and many of those slain for the witness of Jesus, will be Gentiles of every nationality.

The dispensations are totally distinct. When the Lord Jesus is again revealed, when He comes with clouds and every eye sees Him, when He comes to be glorified in His saints, and admired in all them that believe (2 Thess. i. 10), then Israel will be brought back under the new covenant as the wife of Jehovah on earth, betrothed to Him in faithfulness; but the Lamb will have His Bride in the glory. So far from the real Church being on earth, even the counterfeit church—the synagogue of Satan, the harlot of the Beast—will have been utterly abolished from existence, having been destroyed by the ten kings (Rev. xvii. 16).

So that there will be neither the true, nor the false church on earth then. During the first three and a half years, the false church, whose foundations are now being laid, will make an outward profession of Christianity, as Babylon the Great.

When the Man of Sin sets himself up in the temple of God (2 Thess. ii. 4), denying God and Christ, Babylon the Great associates herself with him. Those whom Christ calls the synagogue of Satan (Rev. iii. 9), are those taking Jewish standing, adopting Jewish customs, on the ground of ritual and ceremony, but instead of being God's Church are in reality Satan's synagogue.

The word synagogue, is composed of two Greek words: "sun," together; and "ago," to lead; signifying to lead together, a promiscuous crowd, gathered together by some common interest. Satan's tares are mingled with the wheat now, by and bye they will be gathered together as his synagogue.

The Hope of the Church.

The present hope of the Church is the fulfilment of the promise of Christ in John xiv. 2, 3, "I come again" (present tense), "and will receive you." Christ puts no interval between. He would not have anything between the heart of His believing ones and His coming. The length of time intervening, makes no difference, provided you put no circumstances between. He would have the brightness of this hope before the eye undimmed (1 Thess. iv. 13-18; 1 Cor. xv. 51-54). This is the Church's hope: not the Antichrist, not the great tribulation, not the year-day theory. The sun in the heavens we are told is ninety-five millions of miles distant; if the atmosphere is clear, we see its light too bright for the eye, and feel its warmth; but if you put even a sheet of tissue paper between it and you, its brightness and warmth are obscured. When the Lord said, " I go," " I come again," He foresaw that more than eighteen hundred years would elapse between, as He said in the parable of the talents (Matt. xxv. 19),—"After a long time the lord of those servants cometh." And in Rev. ii. iii. He gives an outline of the Church's history in emblem, and century after century we have seen this history fulfilled. When the Thessalonian believers turned to God from idols, it was to serve the living God, and to wait for His Son from heaven, even Jesus (1 Thess. i. 9,10); there was nothing between. The Church had lost this hope for centuries; but within the last hundred years, the cry has gone out, not that the end of the world has come, not that the day of judgment is at hand. No; but, "The Bridegroom cometh" (Matt. xxv. 6). There is the counterfeit cry, "Antichrist cometh." " Let no man deceive you by any means " (2 Thess. ii. 3-7).

The great apostasy, or Babylon the Great, cannot take place as long as the Holy Ghost as Comforter is in the Church. He lets, that is, hinders and withholds, and so long as the Holy Ghost as the representative of the Lordship of Christ is down here, the Man of sin, the Lawless one, and Antichrist cannot be revealed. But when the work of the Spirit as Comforter is completed, the body of Christ fully formed to be the Bride of the Lamb, and when He as the true Eliezer has presented her to the heavenly Bridegroom, then, as shown by the emblem in Rev. v. 6, the Holy Ghost will begin to act as the seven Spirits of God sent forth into all the earth, with sevenfold energy and power, sealing the elect out of the twelve tribes of Israel as the nucleus of the coming kingdom, and preparing the innumerable company, for the persecution of Antichrist during the great tribulation.

The promise of the Lord Jesus as the Bright and Morning Star (Rev. xxii. 16-20) is, " Surely I come quickly." May all hearts respond, " Even so, come, Lord Jesus."

CHAPTER II.

THE COMING OF THE SON OF GOD.

(1 Thess. i. 9, 10.)

THE Church in Thessalonica, had a distinct experience and attainment. They were marked at their conversion, for the clearness, of their appreciation of the truth of their Lord's return.

They grasped and realized the practical power of this hope. With loins girded, and lamps lit, they were as men who waited for their heavenly Bride-room, the Lord from heaven, realizing the words of Christ, " I go to prepare a place for you, and if I go and prepare for you a place I come again ;" not " I *will* come " (John xiv. 3).

In these two Epistles to the Thessalonians, the Spirit of God by Paul, delights to expatiate on these heart-comforting Truths; every subject He inter-weaves with this golden thread.

The Apostle Paul could write as directed by the
Holy Ghost to the Thessalonian believers, as being
" in God the Father, and in the Lord Jesus Christ."
How is he able to address them thus. He recognized them as elect of God, beloved of God, chosen
in Christ before the foundation of the world, brought
nigh by the blood of the Lamb, regenerated and
sealed by the Holy Ghost, and thus one in Spirit
with the risen Lord in glory.

He had not seen the record of their names in the
Book of Life, but because the word he preached to
them came in power, in the Holy Ghost, in much
assurance (verse 5), he knew they were begotten
again by the Word of Truth, living and abiding for
ever.

The word he brought from God, came in the power
of God, was manifested in their life, character, and
conversation, in their work of faith, labour of love,
and patience of hope (verse 3), which was patent to
all the region round about. They were an epistle of
Christ known, and read of all. What is conversion?
A turning round ; a change of mind, heart, walk,
and action. This proof was manifest in them, they
had turned their back on idols, and their face was
Godward ; their life was a living service to the living God. They were conspicuous for works of faith
and labours of love, but there was another thing
wrought in them by the Spirit of God ; there was
the " patience of hope," and the Holy Ghost Himself

was in them as the Seal and Earnest, and He gave them the foretaste of this "blessed hope."

What was their hope? To die and go to heaven? Truly to depart and be with Christ is far better than continuing here; but their hope was something more definite. It was to wait for the Son of God from heaven.

Not a figurative, but a personal coming, according to chapter iv. 16, the Lord Himself descending from heaven.

It is quite true, the Lord Jesus does often manifest Himself to His departing saints, but this is not the hope here referred to. The Old Testament saints looked for their Messiah, Abraham's Seed, David's Heir; but to us His incarnation, His atoning sacrifice, and ascension, are accomplished facts. We look for the Son of God from heaven.

It is of the utmost importance to notice the precision and propriety, with which the Spirit of God uses the Divine titles, and the distinction which He makes between the title "Son of God" and "Son of Man," though indeed the Person is the same. We wait for the SON OF GOD FROM HEAVEN, not for the SON OF MAN TO THE EARTH. It is the risen Christ we long for, whom God "raised from the dead, even Jesus, our Deliverer from the wrath to come," who comes to receive us to Himself; and to whom we owe our redemption from eternal woe. But if the wrath from which He has redeemed us will be to the lost for ever "the wrath to come;" the glory, the blessedness, and the joy to which He will receive us, will continue throughout eternal ages. It will be still the joy to come, wherein God will show the exceeding riches of His grace in His kindness towards us in Christ Jesus.

CHAPTER III.

THE JUDGMENT-SEAT OF CHRIST.

(2 Cor. v. 10.)

"FOR what is our hope, or joy, or crown of rejoicing? Are not even YE in the presence of our Lord Jesus Christ at His coming? For YE are our glory and joy" (1 Thess. ii. 19, 20).

Similar to this is the language of the Apostle in 2 Cor. i. 14: "As also ye have acknowledged us in part, that we are your rejoicing, even as YE also are ours in the day of the Lord Jesus."

When the Son of God has descended from heaven and has received His saints to Himself, His first action will be to gather them to His judgment-seat, and there take account of His servants; "for we must all appear before the judgment-seat of Christ" (2 Cor. v. 10). Again we read in Rom. xiv. 10, 11, 12, "Why dost THOU judge thy brother? or why dost THOU set at nought thy brother? for we shall

all stand before the judgment-seat of Christ. For it is written, As I live, saith Jehovah, every knee shall bow to Me, and every tongue shall confess to God. So then every one of us shall give account of himself to God." "Because God hath appointed a day, in the which He will judge the world in righteousness by that Man whom He hath ordained " (Acts xvii. 31).

But "one day is with Jehovah as a thousand years " (2 Pet. iii. 8). This day of judgment is not a brief space of four and twenty hours, but consists of successive acts extending over a lengthened period. These separate acts of judgment may be thus enumerated.

First: The Judgment-seat of Christ after the Lord has come for His saints.

Second: His revelation from Heaven in flaming fire, taking vengeance on His enemies, when He appears as Son of Man to take His Kingdom.

Third: When He sits upon the throne of His glory, and the living nations of the earth are gathered before Him (Matt. xxv. 31-46).

Fourth: His judgment of the nation of Israel, according to Psa. L.

Fifth, "The great white throne " at the conclusion of the millennial kingdom (Rev. xx. 11-15).

Our present subject is "THE JUDGMENT-SEAT OF CHRIST." We will first consider the time of this judgment. It is when the Lord comes for His saints, according to Rev. xxii. 12, " Behold, I come quickly; and My reward is with Me, to give every man according as his work shall be."

But who are they who shall appear before Him ? Those, and those only, who have part in the first resurrection, and they appear before Him in their raised and glorified bodies. It is no question of salvation or condemnation, of life or death ; they are already saved, justified, and glorified.

What things are those which will then come under examination? Every deed done in the body, whether good or bad (Eccles. xii. 14 ; 2 Cor. v. 10). As said the Apostle "He that judgeth me is the Lord, therefore judge nothing before the time, until the Lord come, who both will bring to light the hidden things of darkness, and will make manifest the counsels of the hearts ; and then shall every man have praise of God " (1 Cor. iv. 4-5). In fact, every action, word or thought, must all be made manifest before Christ, in the presence of an infinitely holy God, and beneath the scrutiny of the Spirit of righteousness and truth.

But for what purpose is this scrutiny made ? It is to separate the precious from the vile, for then "the fire shall try every man's work of what sort it is " (1 Cor. iii. 13). Then those works which have been wrought by the grace of God, as the gold, those which have been the result of the constraining love of Christ as the silver, those choice fruits of the Spirit, like the precious stones, all these purified from the dross, refined from the alloy, and separated from the fruits of the flesh, will "receive the due recompense of reward." Not one holy action, not one loving word, not one spiritual grace overlooked, or unrewarded in that day.

On the other hand, the wood, the hay, the stubble —all that which is ungodly, un-Christlike, and carnal, will be burnt up; the iniquity forgiven, the transgression removed as far as the east is from the west, and the sin cancelled.

CHAPTER IV.

THE PRESENTATION OF THE RISEN SAINTS TO THE FATHER.

(1 Thess. iii. 11-13).

THESE Thessalonian believers having turned to God from idols to serve the living and true God, and to wait for His Son from heaven (1 Thess. i. 9, 10), Paul looked forward with confidence to the judgment-seat of Christ, when they would be his joy and crown (1 Thess. ii. 19, 20). But he was further anxious, in the fervour of his love towards them, that when they were presented by Christ before His Father, they might be unblemished and complete, and to this end he was desirous to see them again " (1 Thess. ii. 17).

In his prayer he recognises the three spheres of Divine operation. He prays to the God and Father in whose hands are all Providential dealings; and to the Lord Jesus Christ, who is Head and supreme in His Church, opening and no man shutting.

He also recognizes the necessity for the internal work of the Holy Ghost in the soul; hence he further prays, "And the Lord make you to increase and abound in love one toward another, and towards all men, even as we do towards you."

There is no tautology here; it is obviously the Lord the Spirit who is here meant. It is the Holy Ghost who sheds abroad the love of God in the heart, and inspires affection to every child in the family, towards every fellow-believer in Christ, and in philanthropy to all mankind, after the example of the early Church in their fresh baptism of the Holy Ghost, after the pattern of the apostles. He acknowledges this love in them, but he prays that it may abound yet more and more. And this with a definite object, "To the end He (the Lord the Spirit) may stablish your hearts unblameable in holiness before God, even our Father." Thus fulfiling the Divine purpose in the sovereignty of God, who hath chosen believers in Christ before the foundation of the world, that they should be holy and without blame before Him in love (Eph. i. 4): and the object for which Christ died, that He might redeem them from all iniquity, and purify unto Himself a peculiar people, zealous of good works (Titus ii. 14). And this is accomplished by the sanctification of the Spirit through the instrumentality of love; not mere human affection. A love which is not only the fulfiling of the law (Rom. xiii. 10), but the perfection of the Gospel, leading to heart holiness, and the establishment of the heart unblameable therein, not only in the sight of men, but in the sight of God.

There is a distinct period here contemplated : it is "before God, even our Father, at the coming of our Lord Jesus Christ with all His saints."

After the Lord Jesus has come and has raised the dead in Christ, and those who had fallen asleep, and having changed the living saints, and settled every question before His judgment-seat, He will next present them all unto the Father, "before the presence of His glory with exceeding joy" (Jude 24). This will be the accomplishment of the Divine plan, the fulfilment of the sovereign election of God in eternity, the atoning work of Christ in time, and the sanctification of the Spirit fully completed.

It is quite natural when a person first begins to inquire into the truth of "the coming of the Lord," or what is known as "the pre-millennial advent" of Christ, to select a number of passages which appear to speak on the point, and to class them all together, as all relating to the same time and the same event.

This is the most frequent cause of the confusion of ideas, and the diversity of opinion on the subject.

It is of the utmost importance, therefore, to distinguish between the coming of the Lord Jesus FOR His saints at the end of the present dispensation; His presentation of them before His Father, which is the coming here spoken of; and the coming of the Son of Man in manifested glory WITH His saints for the establishment of His millennial reign, after the great tribulation, when He comes with clouds and every eye shall see Him.

CHAPTER V.

THE COMING OF OUR LORD JESUS CHRIST.

(1 Thess. iv. 13, 14).

THERE is no need that a child of God should be ignorant concerning any important truth. In the inspired word, the man of God is thoroughly furnished, both as to doctrine and practice. The Thessalonian believers had apprehended the hope of the Gospel, it had taken possession of their souls. Their hope was on the coming, living Son of God, and this hope had purified their hearts through faith. Some of their friends having "fallen asleep," they were unduly sorrowing, supposing that their loved ones had lost something, or would come short of some blessing. The apostle writes, therefore, to comfort and instruct them on this subject. He

shows them it is a question of fellowship with
Christ, even as it is symbolized in the believer's
baptism, fellowship with Christ in death, in resurrection, and in future glory. By the Pentecostal
Spirit they had been baptized into one body, in
fellowship with the risen Lord in heavenly glory.
They were one in Spirit with their Lord, and hence
if the Spirit of Him that raiseth up Jesus from the
dead dwelt in them, He that raised up Christ from
the dead should also quicken their mortal bodies by
His Spirit that dwelt in them (Rom. viii. 11). And
when Christ, who is their life, shall appear, they
also shall appear with Him in glory (Col. iii. 4),
when He comes to be glorified in His saints, and
admired in all them that believe (2 Thess. i. 10).

Verses 15-17. · "For this we say unto you by the
word of the Lord, that we which are alive and remain unto the coming of the Lord shall not prevent
[anticipate, or go before] them which are asleep.
For the Lord Himself shall descend from heaven
with a shout, with the voice of the archangel, and
with the trump of God : and the dead in Christ shall
rise first : then we which are alive and remain shall
be caught up together with them in the clouds, to
meet the Lord in the air : and so shall we ever be
with the Lord."

The apostle is not here expressing an opinion ;
he is speaking by Divine authority, and as one who
has received special revelation from the Lord on this

point. The expression " We which are alive and remain unto the coming of the Lord," being the participle with the article, designates a class,—we the living and remaining ones.

Paul and these Thessalonian believers were among the living and remaining ones at that time. Believers now, and those who shall be living, when the Lord shall come, belong to the same class.

So far from anticipating, or going before those who have fallen asleep, at the Lord's coming, the dead in Christ will be raised first, before the living saints are changed.

Mark the words: "The Lord Himself shall descend from heaven;" this is no mystical or spiritual coming, but real and personal. And note again, it is not said He shall come to the earth, but that He shall descend from heaven. A time will come, when the Son of Man shall come with clouds, and every eye shall see Him, when His feet will stand on the Mount of Olives; but that is not the event here spoken of. He is now seated at the right hand of God, expecting, till His enemies be made His footstool. But in the interval, while He is waiting for the Kingdom, the Holy Ghost as Comforter is preparing for Him a Bride, the gift of His Father, and the purchase of His blood, to be His companion in His manifested glory, and in His millennial and eternal reign.

When His Bride shall be spiritually perfected, every member written in God's book added, and the whole complete, the Holy Ghost, the Comforter, shall present her to the heavenly Bridegroom, who will come forth in the gladness of His heart, and with a shout, to meet her. He will come from heaven as the Son of God, to receive His bride to Himself, to be with Him where He is, before He comes to the earth as Son of Man, to establish His kingdom. The innumerable company of angels will have fellowship with Him in His joy, and the trump of God adds the expression of Divine majesty and authority.

"And the dead in Christ shall rise first." "The dead in Christ" is a comprehensive term. It includes all who, from righteous Abel, shall up to that period have departed in the faith of Christ, and all who since the martyred Stephen, have fallen asleep in Christ. Including, therefore, those loved ones who had gone from amongst these Thessalonian believers about whom they were so anxious.

"Then we which are alive and remain shall be caught up together with them in the clouds." Then those living and remaining at that period—you and I, if the Lord should come quickly, or those who should succeed us if He tarry—in a moment, in the twinkling of an eye, shall be caught up, after the example of Enoch, the seventh from Adam, who was not found because God had translated him. Two men in one bed, the one taken and the other left;

two in the field, the one taken and the other left; two women grinding at the mill, the one shall be taken and the other left; the wheat gathered into the garner; the good fish gathered into vessels. The servant who shall be found with his hand on the latch to open immediately at the knock of his Master shall receive his Master's blessing. The wise virgins with oil in their vessels shall go in with the Bridegroom, and the door will be shut.

The saints of the former dispensation: those belonging to the church now: and those living and remaining ones at that time, will be caught up together in the clouds, which will receive them out of the sight of men, even as on the day of Christ's ascension a cloud received Him from the upturned gaze of His disciples on the mount of Olives. But, though the clouds will be the gathering place of the saints, there is a higher and a purer joy in reserve. This is preparatory to their meeting the Lord in the air. Not in the obscurity of cloudland, but in the pure ethereal light of heaven, there to see Him as He is, and, as the result, to be conformed to His likeness. By a Divine, spiritual, and heavenly photography, He who is the brightness of the Divine glory, and the express image of His person, will, by an instantaneous process, stamp on the resurrection bodies of His redeemed, His own impress, never to be effaced, but remaining on them through the ages of eternity. And so, associated together in resur-

rection incorruptibility, and conformed to the glorified person of the Redeemer, shall we for ever be
with the Lord.

Wherefore let us comfort one another with these
words. Not terrify one another with dark forebod-
ings of apostasy, the coming of Antichrist, and the
great tribulation, as though the day of Christ, or the
Messiah were at hand; but with this bright and
blessed hope of the coming of the Lord Jesus Christ,
and of our gathering together unto Him.

CHAPTER VI.

THE TIMES AND THE SEASONS.

(1 Thess. v. 1-3).

ONE of the last utterances of our beloved Lord, ere He ascended from this world unto the Father, in answer to the question of His disciples, "Lord, wilt Thou at this time restore again the kingdom to Israel?" was, "It is not for you to know the times or the seasons, which the Father hath put in His own power" (Acts i. 6, 7). It was probably in reference to these and similar words of the Lord Jesus, that the Apostle Paul could say "ye know perfectly." With regard to the coming of the Son of Man, the Lord Himself, in the days of His flesh, told His disciples, "Of that day and hour knoweth no man, no, not the angels of heaven, but my Father only" (Matt. xxiv. 36). "That day" refers to the manifestation of the Son of Man, which ushers in

the day of Jehovah to the world. In Psa. cx. we read,
' Jehovah said unto My Lord, sit Thou at My right
hand until I make Thine enemies Thy footstool."

The Lord Jesus is henceforth expecting the time
when His Father should give Him the kingdom,
according to Psa. ii. 8. "That day" the Father has
kept in His own authority; there the Son was content to leave it; and the Spirit of God says to you
and to me, "It is not for you to know." In the last
chapter of 2 Thess. we read, "The Lord"—that is
the Lord the Spirit—"direct your heart into the
love of God, and into the patient waiting for Christ"
(literally, 'The patience of Christ)." As Christ is waiting and expecting, till the Father's time shall come,
so we are to share that waiting and expectancy
with Him.

The calculation of times and seasons is here expressly forbidden. What has been the outcome of
disobedience to this Divine command? Every former computation has proved false, yet it is done
over and over again. Days are turned into years,
thus falsifying the language of Scripture, and then
calculations are made according to human theories.
It is wiser to leave the times and seasons to Him
who giveth not account of any of His matters.

"The day of the Lord." Here in the original, there
is no article before the title "Lord," which is the New
Testament way of expressing the Hebrew name
Jehovah. This day of Jehovah is that of which the

prophets so frequently spoke, that great day of God Almighty when He will execute His judgments upon an ungodly world. When the ten kings have assembled around Jerusalem and taken the city, when men are in the heyday of apparent success, expecting to have things all their own way, when they shall say, " Peace and safety," when men have avowedly got rid of God and accepted Satan: got rid of Christ, and accepted Antichrist : got rid of the Holy Ghost and accepted the false prophet: effaced from the earth the last trace of the professing church, in the form of Babylon the Great, and are attempt. ing to blot out the name of Israel from the earth ; at that very moment, the sun shall be darkened, the powers of heaven shall be shaken, and then shall be seen the sign of the coming of the Son of Man in heaven. " Then sudden destruction cometh upon them, and they shall not escape."

All these events are connected with the coming of the Son of Man to the earth, not with His coming to receive the Church ; hence says the apostle, "But ye, brethren, are not in darkness, that that day should overtake you as a thief. Ye are all the children of light, and the children of the day : we are not of the night, nor of darkness " (ver. 4-6). But if the Church refuses to walk in the light : is slumbering instead of occupying till the Lord comes, then He says in Rev. iii. 3, " If therefore thou shalt not watch, I will come on thee as a thief, and thou shalt

not know what hour I will come upon thee." Those
Christians who will not watch, but are occupied
with their own dreams of converting the world before He comes, to such His coming will be a surprise,
but a blessed reality, for He will not leave them
behind. On those who belong to Jesus, the true light
now shines : they were sometime darkness, but now
light in the Lord ; by the indwelling Spirit, they are
associated with the risen Christ in heavenly glory.

Just as the moon reflects the light of the sun on
the benighted earth, so the Church, gazing with un-
veiled face, on the glory of God in the face of Jesus
Christ, and transformed by the Lord the Spirit, into
the same image from glory to glory, is called upon
to reflect that light on a world lying in darkness.
And as the lark soars upward at early dawn, and,
singing as she rises, mounts—

> Until the unrisen sun
> Shines on her speckled breast ;

so the Church in Spirit may now hold blest fellowship with her coming Lord.

As risen with Christ we are children of the day,
but as strangers and pilgrims here, we are watching
for " The Morning Star," and, blessed be God, "the
night is far spent and the day is at hand:" " therefore
let us not sleep, as do others ; but let us watch and be
sober. For they that sleep, sleep in the night;
and they that be drunken are drunken in the night.
But let us, who are of the day, be sober, putting on

the breastplate of faith and love, and for a helmet the hope of salvation. For God hath not appointed us to wrath, but to obtain salvation by our Lord Jesus Christ, who died for us, that, whether we wake (watch) or sleep, we should live together with Him" (ver. 6-10). Whether waking, (watching,) or sleeping, or whether holding or not holding certain Advent truths, is not the question. The Church was given to Christ by the Father in eternity, redeemed by the Son of God in time, and sealed by the Holy Ghost until the day of full redemption. All in whom the Spirit of God dwells, when Christ comes, those wise virgins who have oil in their vessels, will go in with Him to the marriage, and then the door is shut.

Therefore let us have grace to obey the exhortation, " Wherefore comfort yourselves together, and edify one another, even as also ye do " (ver. 11). "And the very God of peace sanctify you wholly ; and I pray God, your whole spirit, and soul and body be preserved blameless unto the coming of our Lord, Jesus Christ. Faithful is He that calleth you, who also will do it " (1 Thess. v. 23-24).

CHAPTER VII

THE REVELATION OF THE LORD IN FLAMING FIRE.

(2 Thessalonians i).

THE subject with which the First Epistle to the Thessalonians is occupied, is the coming of our Lord Jesus Christ, and our gathering together unto Him, at the end of the present dispensation; with a word of warning in the fifth chapter, against the calculation of times and seasons. The special subject of the Second Epistle is the manifestation of the Lord as the Messiah, fulfilling the ancient prophecies as to the solemn day of Jehovah, at the end of the age, when the Son of Man comes with clouds, and every eye shall see Him. At the conclusion of the present dispensation, which is that of the Comforter, the good are taken, and the bad are left. But at the end of the age, that is, of "the times of the Gentiles," the evil are taken away and the good are left to possess the millennial kingdom. The end of the world will be at the close of the millennium.

A similar arrangement may be noticed in the parable of the wheat and tares (Matt. xiii. 24-30, 36-43), where the parable itself ends with the gathering of the wheat into the barn, leaving the tares in the field. Whereas the interpretation of the parable gives in addition, the burning up of the tares, the taking out of the kindom all things that offend, and the shining forth of the risen saints as the sun in the kingdom of the Father. So also in the parable of the drag-net and the fishes (Matt. xiii. 47-50): the parable ends with the gathering of the good fish into vessels, corresponding with the removal of the saints ; the interpretation goes on to speak of the severing of the wicked from among the just, and of casting them into the furnace of fire at the end of the age.

The Thessalonian believers were at this time passing through a season of tribulation and persecution, and the Apostle comforts them with the prospect of a time when the scene will be totally reversed. In the world, the Church is to expect tribulation, the old enmity between the seed of the serpent, and the seed of the woman still continues ; but it is a faithful saying, that, if we suffer with

Christ, we shall also reign with Him (2 Tim. ii. 11-12).
The apostles and those who shared tribulation with
them, and those who endure tribulation to the end,
will have rest together, when the Lord Jesus is
revealed in flaming fire, seeing it is a righteous
thing with God to recompense tribulation to the
persecutors; and to the persecuted rest, accounting
them worthy of the kingdom for which they also
suffer. Paul's prayer for them in 1 Thess. iii. 12,
had been answered: their faith had grown exceed-
ingly, and their charity or love abounded. He further prays, that God would count them worthy of
this calling, and fulfil in them all the good pleasure
of His goodness (2 Thess. i. 3, 11).

When the Son of Man is revealed from heaven,
accompanied by the angels of His power, it is for
the execution of vengeance on those who are ignorant
of God, in His divine perfections of righteousness,
holiness, and truth, and who are disobedient to the
Gospel of His grace. Those who in this world had
said unto God, " Depart from us," and who had
trodden under foot the blood of Christ, counting the
blood of His covenant an unholy thing, and had
done despite to the Spirit of His grace, will be "pun-
ished with everlasting destruction from the presence
of the Lord, and the glory of His power." The Son
of Man will be revealed in His own glory, and His
Father's glory, with His angels, and accompanied

with ten thousands of His saints. He shall come to be glorified in His saints, those who had died in the faith of Christ from the beginning (2 Thess. i.10); and to be admired in those who had believed in Him during the present dispensation, in fulfilment of His own prayer in John xvii. 20-23. Each risen saint will be conformed to the glorified body of the Redeemer, and each, like the dewdrops of the morn· ing, reflecting the glory of the Sun of righteousness on that millennial morn, when He arises to flood the world with His glory.

CHAPTER VIII.

THE APOSTASY.

(2 Thessalonians ii. 3).

" LET no man deceive you by any means: for that day shall not come, except there come a falling away first."

There are two events which must intervene between "The coming of our Lord Jesus Christ" for His church, and the day of Christ, when the Son of Man shall appear and every eye shall see Him.

The first of these is " a falling away," literally " the apostasy" of the outward professing Church, from its original standing.

The second is the revelation of the Man of sin. The kingdom of the heavens is likened unto a man which sowed good seed in his field, among which the enemy sowed tares (Matt. xiii. 24). The explanation is this: He that sowed the good seed is the

Son of Man, the field is the world, the good seed are the children of the kingdom, the tares are the children of the wicked one.

At the time of the harvest, the tares are bound in bundles; this process, I believe, is going on now. Various forms of error are associating men together, and binding them fast. There is a lukewarm holding of old-established truths, which are being supplanted by rationalistic opinions, advanced thought, &c. While in the professing Church, there is a turning again to the weak and beggarly elements of a former dispensation, destitute of its reality and power.

The tares having been bound, the wheat will be gathered into the garner. This will be " the coming of our Lord Jesus and our gathering together unto Him," leaving the tares to dry, for the burning at the end of the age.

Similarly the parable of the drag-net teaches, that when it is full it is drawn to shore, the good fish are gathered into vessels, and the bad cast out.

There is now unusual activity in the harvest field, for the night is coming, the storm is gathering, and the Gospel net is being cast into new waters.

A time is coming, when true believers will be gathered home, but when those making a profession without reality, like virgins without oil in their lamps—that is, without the Spirit of God in the hearts—will be left outside the door. Then the faith-

ful servant will enter into the joy of his Lord, but
the unfaithful one will have his portion with the
hypocrites.

In a moment—in the twinkling of an eye—all
who belong to Christ, and are sealed with the Spirit,
will be caught up, and the outward professing
Church, destitute of the Spirit, will be left behind.

Those constituting the true Church of God, having
been removed, the false Church will assume its true
character, as described in Rev. xvii., as Babylon the
Great, becoming as Christ calls it in Rev. iii., " the
synagogue of Satan." This will be the Church of the
future, with its magnificent ritual, and worldly
grandeur.

In Rev. xvii., the angel shows John in vision this
Church of the future, under the symbol of a woman
sitting on a scarlet-coloured beast, decked, or gilded
with gold, and precious stones, and pearls, having a
golden cup in her hand, filled with the abominations
and filthiness of her fornication.

This will be the dominant religion of the day,
usurping authority over the State, and prostitut-
ing to her own purpose all that is Divinely precious,
spiritually excellent, and beautiful. That which
will give the wine of her fornication its intoxicating
power, will be its subtle mixture of the Divine with
the human, the spiritual with the carnal, the heavenly with the earthly, the true and the false; so that
the religious, and even the godly, are in danger of

being carried away. Hence the solemn warning, needful even now, "Come out of her, My people." The mother of harlots is abiding her time; she will tire her head like Jezebel by-and-bye; but her daughters have been on the scene, from the earliest period of Christianity.

After the first three-and-a-half years of Daniel's seventieth week of years, he who will be at the head of the beast on which the woman sits, becomes Antichrist, opposing himself above all that is called God, or is worshipped. Then the apostate church will ally herself with him as the harlot associate of the beast, and instead of being the Church of God, and the Temple of the Holy Ghost, will become "the habitation of devils, and the hold of every foul spirit, and a cage of every unclean and hateful bird" (Rev xviii. 2). This will be the consummation of her falling away, her final apostasy.

And instead of being ready for the coming of Christ, she becomes so abominable, that outraged humanity can endure it no longer, insomuch that ten kings will combine to obliterate the apostate Church from the face of the earth, so that not even the Church's counterfeit will be on the scene, when the Lord comes to take vengeance on the beast and the false prophet.

CHAPTER IX.

THE REVELATION OF THE MAN OF SIN.

(2 Thessalonians ii. 3).

" LET no deceive you by any means, for that day shall not come, except there come a falling away first, and that Man of sin be revealed, the son of perdition."

The second event that must intervene between the coming of the Lord to receive His Church, and the day of Christ, is the revelation of the Man of sin. The time of this revelation of the man of sin, is distinctly foretold in the word of God; hence the apostle could say to these Thessalonian believers, "Remember ye not, that, when I was yet with you, I told you these things?" (v. 5). The period is distinct and limited; it is the last week of the seventy weeks of years spoken of by the prophet Daniel. These seventy weeks are determined, or cut out, upon the people of Daniel, as God's people, and upon the city of Jerusalem, regarded as the holy city, and they run on till the coming of Messiah the Prince, when He comes to take the kingdom.

From the time of the going forth of the commandment to restore and build Jerusalem, B.C. 446 (Neh. i.), until the time when Messiah was cut off, A.D. 33, (to which we must add four years, because Anno Domini commences, not at the birth of Christ, but when He was four years of age, making it 37); 69 of these weeks, or 483 years, were then fulfilled ; 446 and 37 complete the 483 years or 69 weeks.

After the crucifixion of Christ, Israel was no longer regarded as God's people, nor Jerusalem as the holy city ; but, during the interval between the sixty-ninth week and the seventieth, the present Church dispensation comes in, when God is taking from among the Gentiles and from the elect of Israel a people for His Name, and a Bride for His Son. When this work of the Comforter is ended, and the body of Christ completed, then, and not till then, the seventieth week commences. In Dan. ix. 26 we read,"And after the threescore and two weeks (seven weeks having already transpired), shall Messiah be cut off, but not for Himself," literally, " and nothing to Him." From this time onward, Israel is no longer regarded as the people of God, nor Jerusalem as the holy city.

"And the people of the prince that shall come, shall destroy the city and the sanctuary," which was fulfilled by the Roman army under Titus, A.D. 70, or properly 74, thirty-seven years after the death of Christ.

Verse 27. "And He" (the prince that shall come) "shall confirm a covenant with many for one week."

This is the last week of Daniel's seventy weeks of years, of which we are now speaking. When this prince, the Man of sin, comes, it is as head of the Roman Empire in its last form, divided into ten kingdoms. He will be the people's king, the head of the empire of the beast.

He, the "little horn," will make a covenant with Israel for one week of seven years, recognising them as a nation, and as the people of God, to whom David belonged. He will allow them in the providence of God to return to their own land, and will give them Palestine for their possession, and Jerusalem as the metropolis. He will also allow them to have their temple, their sacrifices, and their worship, and will guarantee these privileges to them for seven years. During the first three and a half years, he faithfully keeps his covenant. At this time, he is occupied with the establishment of his kingdom. He comes in peaceably, deceives many, patronising all religions.

At the end of three and a half years he breaks the covenant, takes away the daily sacrifice he had permitted, sets himself up "in the temple of God, shewing himself that he is God" (2 Thess. ii. 4). He sets up the "abomination of desolation" prophesied of by Daniel the prophet (chap. ix. 27) which is referred to by the Lord Jesus (Matt. xxiv. 15).   Now he comes out in his true character, opposing and exalting himself above all that is called God, and sets himself up as the one supreme object of worship on earth, as anti-God and anti-Christ.

During this last week of Daniel's seventy, God will own Israel again as His people, sealing 144,000 of them out of all their tribes (Rev. vii.); and, according to Rev. xi., He will recognize Jerusalem as the holy city, and the temple there, as the temple of God, with its sacrifices and worship, and will raise up the prophetic testimony of His two witnesses in connection with it.   But during the last three years and a half, Jerusalem is compared to Sodom and Egypt (Rev. xi. 8), and will be trodden down of the Gentiles, "until the time of the Gentiles be fulfilled" (Luke xxi. 24).

CHAPTER X.

THE WITHHOLDER.

(2 Thess. ii. 5-8).

" REMEMBER ye not, that, when I was yet with you, I told you these things ? And now ye know what withholdeth (restraineth) that He might be revealed in his (his own) time. For the mystery of iniquity (lawlessness) doth already work: only He who now letteth (withholdeth or restraineth) will let (restrain), until He be taken out of the way (midst). And then shall that Wicked (Lawless One) be revealed, whom the Lord shall consume with the Spirit of His mouth, and shall destroy with the brightness of His coming."

Before the coming of the day of Christ, or the manifestation of the Son of Man in glory, there will take place, as we have seen, the apostasy of the professing Church, and the revelation of the Man of sin. But during this present dispensation, there is something that hinders these previous events, or a restraining power. This was a truth well-known to these Thessalonian believers.

"The mystery of lawlessness" was working, even as early as the Apostle's time ; since then, it has been rapidly developing. In the present day, we see an impatience of control, the exercise of man's self-will, and a demand for liberty and equality. We discover it in the family, school, trade, government, &c., varying in different countries in its outward manifestation, as Democracy, Socialism, Nihilism, &c. Do you know what keeps under control the lawless spirit of the times, and prevents its full manifestation? The same Holy Spirit which rested on Jesus during His sojourn here, and who was sent down as Comforter at Pentecost, is the One whose presence in the Church prevents her apostasy, and who, being with the Church and in the world, maintains the lordship of Christ, until the Church is complete.

In Isa. xi. 1 we read, "There shall come forth a Rod out of the stem of Jesse, and a Branch shall grow out of his roots." In the *Rod* out of the stem of Jesse we see "the Child born" (Isa. ix. 6), the Babe of Bethlehem, David's Son and Offspring, the SON OF MAN. In the *Branch* growing out of his roots, we recognize the Son given (Isa. ix. 6), David's Lord (Matt. xxii. 41-55), the SON OF GOD.

Next we read, "And the Spirit of Jehovah shall rest upon Him, the Spirit of wisdom and understanding, the Spirit of counsel and might, the Spirit of knowledge and of the fear of Jehovah," &c. (Isa. xi. 2-4). In the latter part of verse 4 we read, " He shall smite the earth with the rod of His mouth, and with the breath (Spirit) of His lips shall He slay the wicked " (Lawless One). This is evidently the prophecy alluded to in 2 Thess. ii. 8, "And then shall that lawless one be revealed, whom the Lord shall consume with the Spirit of His mouth, and shall destroy with the brightness of His coming.

Jesus was not only the Root out of a dry ground, the Son of Man ; He was also the Christ, the Anointed One, filled and anointed with the Holy Ghost. And it was by that Spirit which rested upon Him, which was given to Him without measure, that He performed His wondrous work, taught His heavenly truths, offered Himself without spot to God, and in resurrection carries on His work. It is the same Spirit of Truth who is now sent down as Comforter to abide in the Church ; it is this Spirit that we share, it is this power of the Highest resting on us, this presence in the Church which prevents it from becoming utterly corrupt, and restrains the manifestation of the Lawless One.

Very early in the history of the Church, the leaven of false doctrine was inserted by the woman Jezebel (Matt. xiii. 33 ; Rev. ii. 20), and that process of corruption has gone on ever since.

In Zech. v. 6-8 we read of a talent of lead put upon the mouth of the ephah (the ephah is three measures); by and by the talent of lead will be removed, and the apostate church will be fully developed. Then the woman will herself sit in the midst of the ephah.

"This," says the prophet, "is wickedness"—literally lawlessness, or the lawless woman, the feminine of the Lawless One. She will become Babylon the Great of the Book of Revelation.

During the interval between the removal of the Church, and the manifestation of the Son of Man in glory, the Spirit's restraining influence having been removed, the apostasy of the Church will be consummated in Babylon the Great, and the Lawless One in all the energy of Satan will be fully revealed. The Apostate Church will come to her end by the united action of the ten kings, and the kingdom of the beast headed up under the Lawless One, will be destroyed by the manifestation of the Lord in glory.

CHAPTER XI.

THE FALSE PROPHET.

(2 Thess. ii. 9-12).

THE coming of the Lord Jesus Christ to receive His Church, concludes the present dispensation; afterwards the last week of Daniel's seventy weeks of years, completes and ends the age.

During the first three and a half years, Satan will have his counterfeit of God's Church, which Christ calls Satan's synagogue (Rev. ii. 9; iii. 9). During the last three and a half years, she will become the harlot companion of the beast, and the habitation of demons, her abominable character so patent to the whole world, that the ten kings of the Roman empire, will remove every vestige of her, and she will sink like a millstone in the mighty ocean.

In Rev. xvi. 13, 14, we read, "I saw three unclean spirits like frogs come out of the mouth of the dragon, and out of the mouth of the beast, and out of the mouth of the false prophet." This is the trinity of hell. The DRAGON is that old serpent called the Devil and Satan, which means "Adversary" (ch. xii. 9), the enemy of God and man, who during the last three and a half years is cast out of the heavenlies, and with his angels comes down to the earth, exalting himself above the supremacy of GOD THE FATHER. The BEAST is the last form of the Roman Empire, headed up in the Man of Sin, the Lawless One, the son of perdition, who becomes the incarnation of Satan, the Antichrist, the counterfeit of the SON OF GOD. The FALSE PROPHET will imitate the personality, works, and offices of the HOLY GHOST. He will exalt the Antichrist and dragon, instead of Christ and God ; and, energised by Satan, will perform such lying wonders, that Christ said, "If it were possible, they shall deceive the very elect" (Matt. xxiv. 24).

Towards this threefold termination, everything is progressing.

The increase of lawlessness is preparing the way for the establishment and manifestation of THE LAWLESS ONE.

Sacerdotalism, Romanism, and false profession are preparing the way for BABYLON THE GREAT.

Science without God, is preparing for the appearance of THE FALSE PROPHET. It is remarkable, how far critical advanced thought is gaining in this direction, setting aside the authority of GOD in His Word, the atoning sacrifice of CHRIST, and the revealing and teaching of the HOLY GHOST.

Science with all its appliances, cannot find out God, and it denies the possibility of miracles, avowing its disbelief in the supernatural. But, when this dispensation closes, Satan will supply science with supernatural and miraculous power. He whose coming is "after the working of Satan comes with all power, and signs, and lying wonders, and with all deceivableness of unrighteousness,"

The false prophet, the second beast of Rev. xiii. 11-17, will make fire as Elijah did, come down from heaven (which the prophets of Baal could not do); and, he will persuade the dwellers on earth, to make an image to the beast, the Lawless One, which had received the wound by a sword, and did live. "And he had power to give life unto the image of the beast, that the image of the beast should both speak, and cause that as many as would not worship the image of the beast, should be killed;" thus counterfeiting the resurrection of the Lord Jesus.

Now the testimony of the Holy Ghost to the Person, miracles, and resurrection of the Lord Jesus, received on the authority of God, is salvation. Then the lying wonders of the false prophet, wrought in connection with the Antichrist, in the energy of Satan, believed in on his authority, will be inevitable and eternal perdition. A solemn manifestation of the righteous retribution of a holy God. "For this cause, God shall send them strong delusion, that they should believe THE lie : that they all might be damned who believed not the truth, but had pleasure in unrighteousness."

In striking contrast to all this, the apostle continues in his Epistle to the Thessalonian believers, "But we are bound to give thanks always to God for you, brethren, beloved of the Lord, because God hath from the beginning chosen you to salvation, through sanctification of the Spirit and belief of the truth ; whereunto He called you by our gospel, to the obtaining of the glory of our Lord Jesus Christ. Therefore, brethren, stand fast, and hold the traditions which ye have been taught, whether by word, or our epistle. Now, our Lord Jesus Christ Himself, and God, even our Father, which hath loved us, and hath given us everlasting consolation, and good hope, through grace, comfort your hearts, and stablish you in every good word and work."

CHAPTER XII.

THE CHARACTERISTICS OF THE PRESENT DISPENSATION.

(Matthew xxiv. 1, 2).

THIS Temple, to which the disciples called the Lord's attention, was not the original Temple of Solomon, nor that rebuilt in the times of Ezra and Nehemiah; but the Temple erected by Herod the Great, which took forty and six years in building.

It was built of enormous stones, which were visible to the outward sight, unlike the smaller uniform stones of the Temple of Solomon, encased with silver, cedar, and gold, concerning which it was written, " There was no stone seen."

V. 3, "And as He sat upon the Mount of Olives, the disciples came unto Him privately, saying, Tell us, when shall these things be ? and what *shall be* the sign of Thy coming, and of the end of the world" (completion of the age)?

The disciples here ask three questions—First, "When shall these things be?" That is, when these great buildings should be thrown down, and not one stone be left upon another. The Lord's answer to this question is not recorded in Matt. xxiv., nor in Mark xiii., but the Spirit of God gives His reply in full, in Luke xxi. 7, 20, in answer to a similar question. "What sign will there be when these things shall come to pass?" To which the Lord replied, "When ye shall see Jerusalem compassed with armies, then know that the desolation thereof is nigh." This was accomplished in A.D. 70, when Jerusalem and the Temple were destroyed by the Roman armies.

The second question is, "What shall be the sign of Thy coming?" His coming has a twofold aspect: He will come as Son of God to receive His Church and take His Bride—the signs of this coming are spiritual, and only to be spiritually discerned. He also will come as Son of Man, to receive and establish the kingdom, of this coming there will be many visible signs.

The answer to the third question is given in Matt. xxiv. 29, 30. "Immediately after the tribulation of those days, shall the sun be darkened, and the moon shall not give her light, and the stars shall fall from heaven, and the powers of the heavens shall be shaken : and then shall appear the sign of the Son of Man in heaven." This will be at the end, or completion of the age.

From verses four to fourteen, the Lord Jesus gives us the character of this present dispensation, during His absence. Whilst He speaks of His return as the next event to be expected, with nothing between, " I go to prepare a place for you : I come again," to keep His servants on the tip-toe of expectation ; still He has given them to understand it is " after a long time " He comes, to take account of His servants (chapter xxv. 19). They must be prepared to "wait" as well as to " watch."

There are seven particulars to be observed.

First. " Many shall come in My Name, saying, ' I am Christ,' and shall deceive many " (verse 5).

The Apostle John tells us that in his time there were many antichrists (1 John ii. 18); they have characterised the whole period from beginning to end. Perhaps no age has lacked its antichrists, who have usurped the place and prerogative of the Lord Jesus, either as Pope, or something else.

Second. "And ye shall hear of wars and rumours of wars ; see that ye be not troubled, for all these things must come to pass, but the end is not yet " (verse 6). It is not during the present dispensation that men will beat their spears into pruning hooks. The Church is not going to establish a millennium of universal peace, but wars and rumours of wars are to be expected. It has been common to say, when there has been a great war, that the end of the world has come. These things must come to pass, but the end is not yet.

Third. "And there shall be famines." Though God is longsuffering and kind, sending His rain on the evil and on the good, giving fruitful seasons, and filling men's hearts with food and gladness; still, there are times when He makes men feel that they are dependent on Him for their daily bread (verse 7).

Fourth. " Pestilences and earthquakes in divers places." Though there are at the present time so many sanitary arrangements, yet, as in former ages, notwithstanding all, at times pestilences, and epidemics prevail, and earthquakes are of frequent occurrence.

Fifth. Persecutions. The disciples of Christ, for His sake, are hated of all nations. The Gospel has been universally met with persecution, and carried division into families who have betrayed and hated one another (verse 9, 10).

Sixth. False prophets. "And many false prophets shall rise, and shall deceive many" (verse 11). This corresponds with other predictions of the last days of the church, when " perilous times " should

come (2 Tim. iii. 1), when "there shall be false
teachers among you" (2 Pet. ii. 1), concerning whom
the Apostle John said, "Believe not every spirit, but
try the spirits whether they are of God, because
many false prophets are gone out into the world"
(1 John iv. 1). Surely this warning is needed now;
many false prophets and teachers are arising, and
many are being deceived.

Seventh. Lawlessness and lukewarmness. "And
because iniquity (lawlessness) shall abound, the love
of many shall wax cold. But he that shall endure
unto the end, the same shall be saved" (v. 12, 13).
The mystery of lawlessness began to work in the
apostles' time; how much more abounding now!
Is it not pervading all nations? And, as predicted
by our Lord, in the address to the Church at
Laodicea (Rev. iii. 15), another feature of the last
times is indifference to the fundamental truths of
the Gospel, such as the sovereignty of God, the
Divinity and atoning work of Christ, the personality
of the Holy Ghost, and the integrity of God's
Word, even by those who profess and call themselves Christians. Hence the importance of the
words of the Lord Jesus, addressed to the Church
in Philadelphia, "Behold, I come quickly: hold that
fast which thou hast, that no man take thy crown"
(Rev. iii. 11).

Another feature of the approaching end of this dispensation, is increasing activity in the Gospel field.

"And this Gospel of the kingdom shall be preached in all the world for a witness unto all nations; and then shall the end come" (v. 14). This corresponds with the last parable of Matt. xiii., that series of parables which map out the age. The time has come for the drag-net to be let down, there is deep-sea fishing among the dregs of human society, in the depths of poverty and sin. It is the time of harvest, and the Master sees the storms are coming, and is sending out every available hand before the night comes.

CHAPTER XIII.

THE LAST WEEK OF DANIEL'S SEVENTY WEEKS OF YEARS.

(Matthew xxiv. 15).

" WHEN ye, therefore, shall see the abomination of desolation, spoken of by Daniel the prophet."

The prophecy of Daniel to which our Lord refers, is thus recorded in Dan. ix. 27: "And he shall confirm the covenant with many (a covenant with the many) for one week: and in the midst of the week, he shall cause the sacrifice and the oblation to cease, and for the overspreading of abominations he shall make it desolate (and upon the wing abominations making desolate), even until the consummation, and that determined shall be poured upon the desolate " (desolator).

The prince that shall come, whose people (the Roman people) had destroyed the city and the sanctuary (Dan. ix. 26), will be the last head of the Roman empire, the Lawless One, the little horn of Dan. vii. 8. He, in the providence of God, will allow the people of Israel to return to their own land, will acknowledge their nationality as a distinct people, will reinstate them in Jerusalem as their metropolis, will permit them to have their temple and their sacrifices.

Rev. xi. 1, 2, shows that the temple, the altar, and the worship, will be recognised by God, and Jerusalem as the holy city. This cannot take place during the present dispensation. He, the prince, will confirm a covenant with Israel for one week of years, and will guarantee them their national privileges for seven years, but in the midst of the week he will break the covenant, take away the daily sacrifice, and set up the abomination of desolation in the holy place. There is no building on earth now, which can be called " the Temple of God," but then 2 Thess. ii. 4 will be fulfilled, when he, the son of perdition. opposing and exalting himself above all that is called God, will sit in the temple of God.

The first three and a half years of this last seventieth week of years will be occupied by the Lawless One in the establishment of his kingdom, as shown by the vision of the four horses in Rev. vi. 1-8, and the opening of the four seals.

The rider on the white horse, the Lawless One, will not wear the Diadem or royal crown, but the " Stephanos," the Victor's Crown awarded him by the people. He goes forth conquering and to conquer ; the result of which is warfare, symbolised by the red horse, followed by the black horse of famine, and the pale horse of pestilence, and death. Thus the judgments mentioned by the Lord (Matt. xxiv. 1-14), as characterising the present dispensation, will in their exact order follow one another, in that first half of the week. Matt. xxiv. 15 brings us to this period in the half of the week, when the prince, having broken the covenant, will set up the abomination in the holy place ; and, then will begin that fearful persecution of which Daniel and our Lord speak, lasting three and a half years.

The disciples to whom the Lord spoke were the godly remnant of Israel at that time, and as such received instruction for the remnant of the latter day ; hence the Lord addresses them, giving counsel for that time, " Pray ye that your flight be not in the winter, neither on the Sabbath day " (v. 20). He does not say on the Lord's day, but on the Sabbath, recognising the seventh day Sabbath, which will then be strictly observed. It would therefore, be of importance that they should not be obliged to flee on that day.

The reason is given in verses 21, 22 : " For then shall be great tribulation, such as was not since the beginning of the world to this time, no, nor ever shall be. And except those days should be shortened, there should no flesh be saved ; but for the elect's sake those days shall be shortened." This tribulation cannot be referred to any persecution of Christians during the Christian era, for none of them were unparalleled; nor were they connected with the observance of the Jewish Sabbath.

Neither can it refer to the trials and afflictions of Christians extended over the whole period, since it is distinctly limited to a definite time.

This time of "The Great Tribulation" is variously described, that we make no mistake, as time (one year), times (two years and a half), or three years and a half, consisting of forty and two months, or one thousand two hundred and threescore days (not years). During this period, the Lawless One will take the place of God. Satan will be cast out of the heavenlies, and with his angels comes down to the earth, having great wrath. Babylon will be drunken with the blood of the saints; and those who will not worship the beast or receive his mark, but who confess the Christ of God, will be either killed, boycotted, or driven to the ends of the earth. The signs wrought by the false prophet will be so stupendous, and the forces brought to bear so great, that nothing but the sovereign and almighty grace of God, will be sufficient to preserve the souls of men from the strong delusion and its eternal consequences. In the grace of God this state of things is limited to the definite period already mentioned.

"Immediately after the tribulation of those days shall the sun be darkened, and the moon shall not give her light, and the stars shall fall from heaven, and the powers of the heavens shall be shaken: and then shall appear the sign of the Son of Man in heaven: and then shall all the tribes of the earth mourn, and they shall see the Son of Man coming in the clouds of heaven with power and great glory" (ver. 29, 30). These signs in the heavens usher in the august day of Jehovah, spoken of by the ancient prophets, the day of Christ, the manifestation of the Son of Man in power and great glory, when He comes to put down all His enemies, and to establish His millennial kingdom.

"And He shall send His angels with a great sound of a trumpet, and they shall gather together His elect from the four winds, from one end of heaven to the other" (ver. 31). This will be the fulfilment of Isa. xxvii. 13, "And it shall come to pass in that day, that the great trumpet shall be blown, and they shall come which were ready to perish in the land of Assyria, and the outcasts in the land of Egypt, and shall worship Jehovah in the Holy Mount at Jerusalem." This must by no wise be confounded with " the trump of God" 1 Thess. iv. 16 ; nor with the seventh trumpet of Rev. xi. 15. Israel will then be restored to their own land, and the mountain of Jehovah's house will be established upon the top of the mountain, and exalted above the hills, as the centre of worship for Israel and the whole earth, when Jerusalem will become the Holy City, and God's centre of dominion over the whole world.

CHAPTER XIV.

PARABLE OF THE FIG TREE AND THE DAYS OF NOAH.

(Matthew xxiv. 32-42).

THERE is no outward sign connected with the return of the Lord Jesus Christ to receive His people to Himself. The Master of the household has left His house and commanded the porter to watch, and would have His servants wait for their Lord, that they may open immediately to Him, needing no warning. Yet there are tokens of a spiritual nature which we do well to observe. We have an illustration in the fig tree whose branches are brittle in the winter, having no sap, but as spring advances, and the sap rises, the branches are no longer brittle, but become tender and moist, giving evidence of the approaching summer.

We have tokens of the Lord's coming in certain principles which operate slowly at first, but continue to gather strength. Lawlessness, departure from the truth in those who ought to be guardians of the faith, a spirit of delusion and doubt. We see and know that the day of God's longsuffering draws to its close, and the day of vengeance of our God is near, even at the doors. For the Spirit speaketh expressly that in the last days perilous times shall come (see the Epistles of Peter and Jude).

On the other hand, if we take the fig tree as an emblem of the Jewish nation; after the apathy of centuries; the softening of Jewish prejudices and rising inquiry concerning the truths of Christianity, may surely be taken as an encouraging indication that Israel's summer time is nigh at hand, when there shall come out of Zion the Deliverer, who shall turn away ungodliness from Jacob.

Verses 34, 35. "Verily I say unto you, This generation shall not pass till all these things be fulfilled. Heaven and earth shall pass away, but My words shall not pass away."

In the prophetic Scriptures there is often the remarkable feature of a twofold fulfilment, one being more literal and near, the other spiritual and prolonged. So in the verse before us.

The expression "this generation" may be taken in a literal, outward, general sense, of men existing

in a certain age. Literally, the city and the Temple
were destroyed about thirty-seven years after this
prediction. Or, it may be understood in a moral
sense such as, " There is a generation that curseth
their father. and doth not bless their mother " (Prov.
xxx. 11-14).

"An evil and adulterous generation seeketh after
a sign " (Matt. xii. 39). It was in this second sense
in which the Lord Jesus used it, signifying that Jews
and Gentiles will continue the same worldly, Christ-
rejecting people as they were then.

Sooner may the host of heaven be dissolved, and
the heavens rolled together as a scroll, and the
earth be removed, than the words of our beloved
Lord pass away. They were brought to the remem-
brance of the apostles by the Holy Spirit, and
inscribed by Him on the sacred page ; hence the
importance of attending to the warning given in
Rev. xxii. 18, 19.

Verses 36-42. "But of that day and hour knoweth
no man, no, not the angels of heaven, but My Father
only. But as the days of Noah were, so shall also
the coming of the Son of Man be. For as in the
days that were before the flood, they were eating
and drinking, marrying and giving in marriage,
until the day that Noah entered into the ark, and
knew not until the flood came and took them all
away ; so shall also the coming of the Son of Man

be. Then shall two be in the field; the one shall be taken (received) and the other left. Two women shall be grinding at the mill; the one shall be taken (received) and the other left. Watch therefore: for ye know not what hour your Lord doth come."

It is not for us to know the times and the seasons, which the Father has put in His own power; hence the danger of turning days into years, according to the year-day theory, and calculating dates and coming events by that method.

We read in Psa. cx. Jehovah said unto David's Lord, "Sit Thou on My right hand, until I make Thy foes Thy footstool." Meanwhile He is waiting in expectancy, until His enemies be put beneath His feet, and the kingdoms of this world become His (Psa. ii.) But, whilst He is waiting for His throne and His kingdom, there is another object of expectancy still dearer to His heart. He is waiting for His Bride, composed of all those who have been given Him by the Father in the counsels of eternity, for whom He has laid down His life, and who are now being prepared by the Comforter.

The parable of the days of Noah is twofold in its application. Two periods are mentioned. The days which were before the flood, which are connected with the world; and the day when Noah entered into the ark, when the eight elect souls were shut in by God. And we find from Gen. vii. that a period of seven days elapsed after Noah entered in before the flood. Strikingly suggestive of the last week of Daniel's seventy weeks which will intervene between the removal of the Church and the execution of judgment on the world.

As in the days which were before the flood, when the Spirit of God was striving with men, they took no heed of the prophecies of Enoch and Noah, reckoning upon the uniformity of nature, which showed no sign of change; so in these last days there are mockers saying, " Where is the promise of His coming ? " (2 Pet. iii. 3-7).

And even the fulfilment of His promise, to come and receive His own, will leave men pursuing the same worldly course, until a more fearful deluge than water will overtake them. "So shall also the coming of the Son of Man be," it will find the world unprepared.

Concerning the time which corresponds with the day when "Noah entered into the ark," the Lord said, "Then shall two be in the field; the one shall be taken, and the other left. Two women shall be grinding at the mill; the one shall be taken and the other left."

The coming of the Lord to receive His own will be simultaneous throughout the whole world; it may be midnight in one part, two men sleeping in one bed, the one taken, caught up to meet the Lord in the air, the other left (Luke xvii.34). It may be midday in another, two men labouring in the field, the one taken, the other left ; in another quarter it may be the early morn, two women preparing the daily meal, the one taken to be for ever with the Lord, the other left with the prospect of the times of Antichrist and the great tribulation.

The Lord foretells that the world will continue its heedless course, as in the days of Noah, up to the time of His coming to take His Church ; and after that, without heeding the warning given, will continue the same worldly career, until for the execution of judgment the Son of Man shall come. But to His waiting, believing people, who are expecting His return, to them His word of exhortation is, " Watch, therefore ; for ye know not what hour your Lord doth come."

CHAPTER XV.

PARABLES OF THE HOUSEHOLDER AND OF THE SERVANTS.

(Matthew xxiv. 43-51).

THIS parable has a threefold application,

First and properly to the world, and not to the Church.

Secondly, to the Church when in a worldly and unwatchful condition.

Thirdly, to the faithful remnant in the later-day trial.

Here the goodman of the house is not the Lord Jesus, but it is a simile drawn from a householder who was not aware when the thief would come, and had neglected to prevent his house from being broken into.

We know from 1 Thess. v. 4-5, that this parable, properly speaking, does not apply to the Church. The apostle there says, " Ye, brethren, are not in darkness, that that day should overtake you as a thief. Ye are all the children of light, and the children of the day ; we are not of the night, nor of darkness." Hence the application is not as in verse 42 : " Watch therefore, for ye know not what hour your Lord doth come : " but it is rather, " Be YE also ready: for in such an hour as ye think not, the Son of Man cometh," similar to v. 39. It is the coming of the Son of Man to the world lying in darkness and worldly security ; when men are saying, " Peace and safety," then sudden destruction comes to them to break up their vision of security and peace.

The expression " Coming of the Lord," is in Scripture connected with His coming for the Church ; and " The coming of the Son of Man " with His appearing to Israel and to the world. It is important to attend to this distinction.

Secondly, it may have an application to the Christian Church when in a worldly condition, and in an unwatchful state.

The Lord Jesus sends the word of warning to the Church at Sardis (Rev. iii. 3): " If, therefore, thou shalt not watch, I will come on thee as a thief, and thou shalt not know what hour I will come upon thee." This applies specially to the time of the

Protestant Reformation and onward. If Christians are found in an unwatchful condition, the coming of their Lord will be as unexpected to them as the coming of the Son of Man will be to the world. If they are saying the coming of the Lord is spiritual and not personal, and at the end of the millennial period and not pre-millennial, while they are dreaming of leavening the world with Christianity, and converting it by the preaching of the Gospel; this unexpected return will " break up " their organizations, and put an end to their vast schemes; nevertheless God will accomplish His own purposes, and establish His kingdom in His own way.

Thirdly. In the time of the great tribulation, at the pouring out of the sixth vial, Christ addresses this word of encouragement to the faithful, persecuted, and tried saints, just previously to His manifestation as the Son of Man in the clouds of heaven. "Behold, I come as a thief. Blessed is he that watcheth, and keepeth his garments, lest he walk naked, and they see his shame" (Rev. xvi. 15.)

Verse 45-47.—" Who then is a faithful and wise (prudent) servant, whom his lord hath made ruler over (set over) his household, to give them meat in due season ? Blessed is that servant, whom his lord when he cometh shall find so doing. Verily I say unto you, that he shall make him ruler over (set him over) all his goods."

A large question is suggested here for consideration; it requires an answer from the servant, and those of the household under his rule.

A " servant," that is a bond or bought servant, one who is entirely the property of his master, conscious that he is not his own, but bought with a price, and constrained by the love of Christ to live unto Him who died for him and rose again.

" Faithful : " for it is required in stewards that a man be found faithful, not justifying himself, but committing himself to Him who judgeth righteously (1 Cor. iv. 1-5).

" Wise or prudent." Not unwise, but understanding what the will of the Lord is, and guiding his affairs with discretion.

" Whom the Lord hath set over his household." A man under authority and conscious that he is not only placed in his office by Divine authority, but sustained in the exercise of it by Almighty power.

It is very important that those who have a gift should recognise it. It is not humility to deny it, whether it be the gift of an evangelist, pastor, or teacher ; but like the faithful servant to say, ''Lord, Thou deliveredst unto me five talents, I own my responsibility to Thee, and to those over whom I am set."

Moses was faithful in God's house as a servant, but Christ as a Son over His own house, whose house are we (Heb. iii. 5, 6); and the servant is appointed to give meat to the household, or, according to Luke xii. 42, " to give them their measure of wheat (margin) in due season." And as Joseph commanded his steward, " Fill the men's sacks with food, as much as they can carry " (Gen. xliv. 1).

There should be oversight and rule in the Church of God, and it is to be recognised, as writes the apostle, " We beseech you, brethren, to know them which labour among you, and are over you in the Lord, and admonish you ; and to esteem them very highly in love for their work's sake " (1 Thess. v. 12, 13). Again, "Let the elders that rule well be counted worthy of double honour, especially they who labour in the word and doctrine " (1 Tim. v. 17). And again, in Heb. xiii. 17, " Obey them that have the rule over you, and submit yourselves: for they watch for your souls, as they that must give account."

The servant in Christ's household here, whether evangelist, pastor, or teacher, is training for higher service and for a nobler ministry. He will not cease to serve, but will enter on a sphere of service wide as the universe, and lasting as eternity. Having been found faithful in a few things, he will be made ruler over many things, and enter into the joy of his Lord.

Verses 48-50.—" But and if that evil servant shall say, in his heart, My lord delayeth his coming; and shall begin to smite his fellow-servants, and to eat and drink with the drunken; the lord of that servant shall come in a day when he looketh not for him, and in an hour that he is not aware of, and shall cut him asunder (cut him off, or severely punish), and appoint him his portion with the hypocrites; there shall be weeping and gnashing of teeth."

When the Lord Jesus comes to receive His own, and to acknowledge the services of His faithful servants, who will together be caught up to meet Him in the air, then those who are servants by profession only, but destitute of the Spirit of Christ, will be left behind. This will involve their being cut off from the privileges of the Christian Church. For after the removal of those real believers who are alive and remain when their Lord comes, there will be no true Church of God on the earth. The outward shell of professing Christianity, destitute of life and spiritual power, will become an apostate Church, consummated in Babylon the Great.

These evil servants may or may not profess the doctrine of what is called the Lord's Second Advent, but in heart they have no desire for His return. They may have hearkened to the voice of the charmer, see Prov. vii. 6-20, finding it convenient to calculate times and seasons, and thus to put off the day of His coming; meanwhile making the most of the present time for worldly, ambitious, and selfish ends.

On such, the day of the Lord will come as a thief in the night, leaving them to take their portion with hypocritical professors, without hope of recovery, in unavailing sorrow and regret.

CHAPTER XVI.

PARABLE OF THE TEN VIRGINS.

(Matthew xxv. 1-13).

THE word " then " connects this parable with the preceding one, in which the Lord speaks of His return ; but in this parable he takes a comprehensive view of the whole period of His absence in one particular aspect. The term " kingdom of heaven," or more properly " the kingdom of the heavens," is peculiar to the Gospel of Matthew. In the other Gospels it is spoken of as " the kingdom of God."

" The mystery of the kingdom of the heavens " relates to the whole period in which Christ, born King of the Jews, rejected by His people Israel, who refused to have Him to reign over them, is now seated with the Father on His throne in the heavens.

One similitude of this kingdom is given by the Lord in this parable ; it is compared to the ten virgins, five of whom were wise and five foolish, as representing all those who own Him as Lord, and are expecting His return.

Christendom, or Christ's kingdom, is now composed of those who acknowledge Israel's rejected King, from the time when Messiah was cut off at the end of the sixty-ninth week, till the commencement of the seventieth week of Daniel's prophecy.

"And went out." The Lord here goes back to the commencement of the dispensation when, as we read in 1 Thess. i. 10, the early disciples turned to God from idols, to serve the living and true God, and to wait for His Son from heaven.

The whole professing Church is represented by the ten virgins, five wise and five foolish. In most of the Lord's parables we find the same twofold division, as the wheat and tares, the good and bad fish, the faithful and unfaithful servants.

What characterised the foolish virgins is, that they took the lamp of profession, acknowledging the Lordship of Christ, and the hope of His return, but were destitute of spiritual reality and power. "They took no oil with themselves." Oil is the emblem of the Holy Spirit, the unction from the Holy One. The foolish take the lamp of profession first, but neglect the oil; the wise, on the other hand, make the possession of the oil in the vessel the first concern (the vessel is the heart), realising the indwelling of the Holy Ghost and His testimony within ; to this they added the outward profession of the hope of His return.

Verse 5. " But while the bridegroom tarried, they all slumbered (grew sleepy) and slept."

The Lord foresaw and foretold this delay, as He says in verse 19, "After a long time the lord of those servants cometh, and reckoneth with them."

He would have His disciples wait as well as watch, but the Church was not prepared for this prolonged delay, which has extended already over eighteen hundred years. The Ephesian Church early lost its first love, the love of its espousals ; and the doctrine of a spiritual coming and reign, instead of a personal and real, early changed the character of the believer's hope. The dark age was the time of profoundest slumber to the whole professing Church, but even since the time of the Reformation, the Church has been dreaming of converting the world previous to, and independent of, her Lord's return.

Previously there had been many cries, such as, the end of the world had come, or the great day of judgment was coming, or the kingdom was going to be set up. Now it is, " Behold, the bridegroom cometh." Behold ! Take notice. Mark well.

It is not Antichrist, nor the great tribulation, but it is the coming of Christ in His especial character as Bridegroom to receive His church before He comes to take the kingdom. This is His coming as the Morning Star, before He rises as Sun of Rightousness on the world. It is within the present century that this testimony has gone forth.

It is not to be received simply as a doctrine, but as a practical truth, for " he that hath this hope on Him (that is Christ) purifieth himself even as He is pure " (1 John iii. 3). It is designed to separate from everything that would be inconsistent with the expectation of meeting Him, that we might be found of Him in peace, without spot and blameless.

The doctrine of the Bridegroom's coming may be discussed and reasoned about, but apart from the supply of the Spirit of Christ, the consideration will lead to no practical or permanent result.

There may be a transitory excitement, but it will soon pass off. The foolish virgins are conscious of this ; " our lamps go out," we cannot keep them burning. The torch-bearers in the east are furnished with a vessel from which they pour a fresh supply of oil, from time to time, and thus keep up the light. Those who possess the Spirit are conscious they have only a sufficiency for themselves. Hence they say, " Go ye rather to them that sell, and buy for yourselves."

Who are those that sell ? Jehovah is the fountain of living waters (Jer. ii. 13 ; Rev. xxi. 5-7)

The fulness of God is treasured up in Christ (John vii. 37-39). He who communicates it is the Holy Ghost (Isa. lv. 1-3), who invites to buy without money and without price.

Solemn lesson. Whatever profession there may be, if there is not the oil in the vessel when the Lord comes, the door will be shut, for "if any man have not the Spirit of Christ, he is none of His." When Christ comes, it is to gather the wheat into the garner, not the tares. Those who in the parable had only the lamp of profession sought an entrance, but the Lord said, "I know you not."

Christ cannot be known apart from the revelation of God by the Holy Ghost. Those cannot know Him, who have not sought the Spirit of revelation, by whom alone He can be truly known, and such at last will be disowned by Him. May the Lord the Spirit direct our hearts into the Love of God, and into the patient waiting for Christ (2 Thess. iii. 5).

CHAPTER XVII.

PARABLE OF THE TALENTS.

(Matthew xxv. 14-30).

THIS is a parable of the kingdom during the present dispensation, wherein the Son of Man, instead of sitting on the throne of His glory (verse 31), is gone to receive for Himself a kingdom, and meanwhile is seated on the throne of His Father in heaven, the "far country" alluded to in the parable. The servants here are recognised as the personal property of their Lord; they are His bought or bondservants, agreeably with Matt. xiii. 44, for the Son of Man has purchased the field, that is, the world and all its contents, so that professors, as well as real Christians are the property of the Lord; hence the possibility of apostates "denying the Lord that bought them" (2 Pet. ii. 1). So likewise the goods which He delivers to His servants are designated as " His goods," they are things connected with His grace, redemption, and Lordship.

According to some, a talent of silver was about £187 10s., but, according to Jewish calculation, about £342 8s. 9d., and the talents are not to be regarded as natural qualifications, such as for music, painting, &c. The lord delivered to his own servants his personal goods; to one he gave five talents, to another two, to another one. By the one talent we may understand those outward privileges and advantages which are the common possession of all professed Christians, including the means of grace, the Lord's day, and an open Bible. By the two talents may we not recognise the communication of spiritual life and divine grace within, in addition to the external means of grace?

Sir Walter Scott recognised this in his well-known lines on the Bible :—

> Within this awful volume lies
> The mystery of mysteries ;
> Happy the man and blest his case
> To whom his God has given grace
> To read, to meditate, and pray,
> To lift the latch, and force the way,
> But better he had ne'er been born
> Who reads to doubt, or reads to scorn.

As the Lord Jesus said to His disciples, " It is given unto you to know the mysteries of the kingdom of the heavens, but to them it is not given." And the Apostle Paul recognises still further gift when he says, " unto you it is given in the behalf of Christ, not only to believe on Him, but also to suffer for His sake." May we not understand by the five talents, not only the outward Christian privileges common to all, and the inward spiritual grace rendering them vital, but, in addition, the special gifts of the evangelist, pastor, and teacher, for testimony, oversight, and service? These special gifts involve corresponding responsibilities, for " to whom much is given, from him shall be much required."

Some may be called, in the providence of God, to serve in a threefold capacity. Timothy, though by gift a teacher, was to do the work of an evangelist, he had also to watch over the flock. The Lord does not overlook natural capabilities, and constitutional capacities in the distribution of His gifts for service. To one who is required to go forth as an EVANGELIST, there is needed hardihood of frame and power of voice. A PASTOR should have a large heart, warm affections to enter into, and feel for, the variety of experiences of the flock. The TEACHER requires to be spiritually-minded, so as to enter into the secret place of the Most High, to understand the mind of God, and with ability to communicate it to others ; hence it is said, " To every man according to his several ability."

We learn from the corresponding parables in Mark xiii. 33-37 and Luke xii. 35-40 that, while the Lord had apportioned to each of His servants their work during His absence, He had left a commandment that a strict watch should be observed, so that when He returns, at whatever hour of the day or watch of the night, they may be ready to open unto Him immediately. He at the same time instructed them to wait patiently, as well as watch vigilantly.

And while His last words were " Surely, I come quickly " (Rev. xxii. 20), and He gives no intimation of anything between, yet He would have His servants prepared for a prolonged delay ; hence He says "After a long time the Lord of those servants cometh, and reckoneth with them." After the Lord has come and received His saints He takes an account of their services, for " we must all appear before the judgment seat of Christ, that every one may receive the things done in his body according to that he hath done, whether it be good or bad " (2 Cor. v. 10).

Those to whom most is committed are the first to be taken account of, for " to whom much is given, of him much shall be required." The servant acknowledges the authority of his lord and the amount of his responsibility to him, " Lord, thou deliveredst unto me five talents." Those to whom the Lord has committed the gift either of evangelist, pastor, or teacher should be ready to acknowledge their accountability, as men under authority, and as stewards of whom it is required that they be found faithful.

Whatever grace or gift is committed to us it is capable of being doubled in value. The Lord entrusts His gifts to be traded with and increased.

Diligence and faithfulness connected with the few things committed to our stewardship in time is a preparation and apprenticeship for more important service in the eternity which lies beyond. Faithful service to the Lord on earth may involve being a partaker of Christ's sufferings, but " it is a faithful saying, if we suffer we shall also reign with Him." In the presence of God is fulness of joy, at His right hand are pleasures for evermore ; for the joy set before Him, Christ endured the cross and despised the shame. This joy He invites the faithful servant to enter into and share with Him.

With regard to the servant who received the two talents (verses 22, 23), it is virtually the same. Grace as well as gift may be multiplied and increased, and the humblest believer may walk so faithfully as to receive from the Lord when He comes His full commendation.

Although the time when the unprofitable servant gives in his account, is when the Lord cometh, yet we know, from other Scriptures, that he does not appear like the faithful servant before the judgment seat of Christ.

Though he professed to know his lord, yet his language shows that he had no real acquaintance with him. Even a child when taught by the Spirit forms a far different estimate of Christ. And every one who has had any real experience of His service has proved that He is meek and lowly in heart, His yoke easy, and His burden light; far from being unreasonable and exacting, that He is the best of masters, and his service perfect freedom.

The outward ordinances of Christianity may be observed, and its essential doctrines intellectually believed, yet the individual may remain unregenerate and unsaved. Through carnality and worldliness the talent may be, as it were, buried in the earth, though not without some effort of mind and struggles of conscience. True faith trusts and confides, but unbelief is fearful and unfruitful.

The Master convicts the unprofitable servant out of his own mouth. Who are the exchangers or bankers referred to by our Lord? May we not understand that, apart from the blessing of God the Father, the grace of the Lord Jesus, and the regenerating and sanctifying power of the Holy Ghost, the outward privileges and doctrines of the Gospel will remain ineffectual; but where the blessing of the Triune God is sought and obtained, the interest will be forth-coming in eternity, in everlasting praise? Thus the Master will receive His own with interest.

The law of the kingdom is, to him that "hath shall more be given, but from him that hath not shall be taken away, even that which he hath," while the unprofitable servant is cast into outer darkness, "where there is weeping and gnashing of teeth."

May we have grace to occupy till He come, "steadfast, unmoveable, always abounding in the work of the Lord," that we may be found of Him in peace, without spot and blameless.

CHAPTER XVIII.

THE JUDGMENT of the LIVING NATIONS.

(Matthew xxv. 31-46).

THE word " But," which is in the original, con-
trasts this parable with the two preceding
ones. Those refer to what takes place when the
Lord comes for His saints; this relates to the time
when He will be manifested as Son of Man with
them. God has appointed a day in which He will
judge the world in righteousness, by that Man whom
He hath ordained; for unto Him every knee shall
bow, and every tongue confess. But we must not
be ignorant of this one thing, that one day is with
Jehovah as a thousand years. The day of salvation
has already extended over eighteen hundred years;
even so the day of judgment will extend over a
lengthened period. Scripture speaks of five distinct
scenes of judgment.

First, the judgment seat of Christ, before which we must all appear when He comes to take account of, and to reward His servants.

Second, when He is revealed from heaven in flaming fire, taking vengeance on them which know not God, and obey not the Gospel, when Antichrist and the false prophet will be destroyed.

Third, the judgment of the nation of Israel as God's people, according to Psa. 1. Psa. li. is, prophetically, Israel's response.

Fourth, the judgment of the living Gentile nations, according to this parable.

Fifth, the judgment of the great white throne, before which all the dead will stand who have not had part in the first resurrection (Rev. xx. 11-15).

Verse 33. When the Son of Man shall sit on the throne of His millennial kingdom, Israel having been restored and settled in their inheritance, the living Gentile nations will come under His discriminating eye ; not that they will be gathered together into one place, for we must remember that this is a parable.

Under the persecutions of Babylon the Great, and especially during the great tribulation under Antichrist and the false prophet, those who acknowledge God and Christ will be either slain, driven out, or scattered among all the nations of the earth. When the Son of Man comes, these nations will be judged according to their treatment of these persecuted ones whom the Lord here acknowledges as His brethren. The reception of these living witnessess by those who ministered to them, will be virtually regarded as the acknowledgment of God, of Christ, and of the Holy Ghost, whereas the rejection and neglect of these outcast ones will be condemned as a participation with Satan, Antichrist, and the False prophet.

The King having divided between them, and placed the righteous on His right hand, the place of favour and approval, He thus addresses them, "Come, ye blessed of My Father, inherit the kingdom prepared for you from the foundation of the world." The King having come to take His kingdom, to receive the heathen for His inheritance, the uttermost parts of the earth for His possession, to sway His sceptre over all the earth, will call on those who are blest of the Father, to take possession of the kingdom prepared for them from the foundation of the world.

He does not say " before " but " *from* the foundation of the world ; " it is the earthly millennial kingdom they are called to inherit. A cup of cold water given to a disciple now will not lose its reward ; but, though the principle is the same, there is something more here : it is the acceptance or rejection of the brethren of Christ during the three and a half years in that crisis of the earth's history.

Verses 41, 46. Those who took part with Satan in the last decisive conflict, must be content to share with him his everlasting portion.

The lake of fire was not originally prepared for man, but for the devil and his angels. But those who in time have said unto God, " Depart from us, for we desire not a knowledge of Thy ways," must not be surprised if they hear the echo come back, "Depart from Me." Those who are blest of God enter the millennial kingdom in possession of everlasting life; for them death is swallowed up in victory.

Although this promise is quoted in 1 Cor. xv. 54, and applied to those who have part in the first resurrection; yet, as originally given, it refers to those nations who are blessed of God during the millennial period, and to Israel as God's people then. See Isa. xxv. 6-8. Hos. xiii. 14.

THE PERFECTIONS
AND EXCELLENCIES OF
HOLY SCRIPTURE

The Perfections and Excellencies

of

Holy Scripture

THOMAS NEWBERRY

The Perfections and Excellencies of Holy Scripture.

Introduction.

"FROM a child, thou hast known the Holy (Sacred)* Scriptures, which are able to make thee wise unto salvation, through faith which is in Christ Jesus. All Scripture is given by inspiration of God, and is profitable for doctrine, for reproof, for correction, for instruction in righteousness: that the man of God may be perfect, throughly furnished unto all good works" (2 Tim. iii. 16, 17). *"Sacred Scriptures," that is, temple or priestly Scriptures; Scriptures for priestly use; written by the

---

* The word here rendered "Holy" in the A. V. is not the ordinary word or holy, but another Greek work signifying "Sacred."

inspiration of God, to be used in the presence of God, by those who have an unction from the Holy One to know all things. "Sacred Scriptures;" only to be understood in God's own light; only to be realised by the teaching of the Holy Spirit—the communication to men of the mind of God, the heart of the Father, in the Person of Christ, and by the Holy Spirit. "Sacred Scriptures," whose source is God the Father, whose subject-matter is the Person of Christ the Son, and the Communicator of which is the Spirit of God. The mind of God in Christ, the glory of God in the Person of Christ, are here revealed, and, as the sun is only seen by its own light, so only may the word of God be apprehended by the teaching of that Spirit, who searcheth all things, yea, the deep things of God. It is the glory of God, in the Person of Christ, that is the object in the mind of God, but the one centre, of this inspired word is the atoning work of Christ— God's centre thought for all eternity. Even as the Tabernacle in the wilderness was the centre of the encampment of Israel, and in the court was the altar of burnt offering, and just as in the courts of the Temple, as described by Ezekiel, the centre will be occupied by the altar of burnt or ascending-offering, in the very centre of Immanuel's land. All the tribes will be stationed above and below the holy oblation, and in the centre of the priests' portion, is the altar of burnt or ascending-offering, with its fire ever burning, the wood ever on the fire, and the sweet savour of the spotless Lamb ever ascending.

But not only is the altar the centre of earth, the centre of Immanuel's land, but the Lamb on the throne is the centre of Heaven; it is the Lamb on the altar below, the Lamb on the throne above, a Lamb as it had been slain. We need to have God's thoughts about that grand, and glorious, and blessed work of the Atonement of our Lord and Saviour Jesus Christ. Redemption by the blood of the Lamb, was in the Father's thought from all eternity, not only as a remedy brought in after ruin. Those who are chosen in Christ, were chosen in Him before the foundation of the world. God, before He created anything, before He brought this universe into being, foresaw in the depths of His infinite mind, that apart from Himself, the relation between creation and Creator could not always stand. God, before He brought a creature into being, made in the counsel of His own Divine mind, in the depths of His own infinite heart, a provision for what would come to pass. Thus, the centre thought of God, is Redemption through the blood of the Lamb. Redemption : not simply the salvation of souls of men, but the purpose of God in atonement, is the security of the universe, throughout all its boundless expanse, throughout all the unreckoned ages of eternity. The purpose of God's heart is declared in this word, "That in the dispensation of the fulness of times, He might head up in one, all things in Christ, things in Heaven and things on earth" (Eph. i. 10). " Having made peace through the blood of His Cross, by Him (that is the spotless Lamb) to reconcile all things unto Himself, whether things on earth, or things in Heaven" (Col. i. 20).

Sin not only came into the world, but the creation has been defiled by the sin of angels. God made a provision in the Incarnation, whereby the creature and creation are linked to the throne of the Almighty, Eternal God. He also provided redemption through the blood of the Lamb, thereby reconciling things in heaven, as well as things on earth.

The divine glory, which is unfolded in the Scriptures, was manifested in Christ, and was foretold and fore-shadowed in the Old Testament types. The experiences of the incarnate Son of God, while hanging on the accursed tree, are brought out especially in the Psalms ; while the wondrous truths connected therewith in the purposes of God, and founded thereon, are revealed in the Prophets. The fulfilment of these types and shadows is given us in the Gospels, the doctrines founded on that atoning work in the Epistles, while the full and finished fruit of Redemption is brought out in Revelation. The roots of this truth, so to express it, run down and ramify in the Pentateuch ; the trunk is seen in the Historical books ; the heart or core, in the Experimental Portions, from Job to Solomon's Song ; the branches spread out in the Prophecies ; the foliage and flowers come out in the New Testament Scriptures, and the finished fruit is shown in the book of Revelation. It is a marvellous whole, one thought running from beginning to end. Every well-bound book is held together by threads which are hidden beneath the cover ; so with this sacred volume. There are lines of Divine truth which run through every portion, and unite the whole together.

Arrangement of the Books of Scripture.

The Sacred Scriptures naturally divide into six distinct portions. The first is—the Pentateuch, or five books of Moses; and the subject there, is THE WORLD AND THE WILDERNESS. The next, or historical portion, is from Joshua to Esther, and the subject is the LAND AND THE KINGDOM. The third, or experimental portion, we find from Job to Solomon's Song; this inner kernal, or core of Scripture, is adapted to man's inward need, giving the experience of COMMUNION RESTORED, and of FELLOWSHIP IN THE SPIRIT, with the Bridegroom of the soul. The next natural division is in the prophetic books— Isaiah to Malachi, all the prophecies. Then we come to the New Testament, and the fifth natural division will be—The Four Gospels; there it is CHRIST ON EARTH. Then from Acts to Revelation is the last division, and there it is CHRIST IN HEAVEN.

While we thus divide the Old and New Testaments into four and two respectively, the New Testament may also be divided into four, corresponding with the four parts of the Old. The four Evangelists will correspond with the five books of Moses—CHRIST ON EARTH; the book of Acts will correspond with the historical portion from Joshua to Esther—CHRIST IN HEAVEN; then the Epistles with the experimental portion, Job to Solomon's Song; and the book of the Revelation with the prophecies, from Isaiah to Malachi.

The Language of Scripture.

The Old Testament, with the exception of a brief portion in Ezra and Daniel, was written in Hebrew, and the New Testament in Greek. Why? Can we discover a reason for this?

The Hebrew language, more completely than any other, is in harmony with the mind of the Eternal and Triune God. And these Hebrew Scriptures present the thoughts of God more completely and perfectly, than they could, if written in any other language.

The Greek, on the other hand, is more adapted to the mind of man. No language could be named, which is more fitted as a vehicle to convey communication from the Divine mind, brought down to us. In the Greek, the wondrous utterances of God are brought easily and exactly within reach of the human mind. The aptitude of thought and expression, and the largeness of the Divine mind is expressed by the Hebrew language, while the infirmity of the human mind is met by the Greek.

God has magnified His word above all His Name, and it is in this word that the Name of God is told out.

Titles of God.

THERE is more importance to be attached to the precise terms and Titles, by which God has been pleased to reveal Himself to man, than perhaps we are in the habit of attaching to them. Each of the Divine Titles is expressive of God, in one or another particular of His Person, character, or attributes. The Spirit of God is very exact in His use of Titles, each being used with a wise and special purpose.

In the first verse of the Bible, God is announced to man as the Triune God, Father, Son, and Holy Ghost, eternally one God, yet in three distinct PERSONS. The word used is *Elohim*, the plural title of God. There is necessity for that. It is the Triune God that speaks in the language of the Old Testament

When the law was given on Sinai, it was the law of
God,—Father, Son, and Holy Ghost. When the glory
of the eternal, invisible God was revealed by Angelic
ministrations, it was the glory of the Three in One.

I fear there is a great deal of Arianism in the
present day, undetected and unsuspected.

For example, when we read in the first chapter of
the Gospel by John verse 18, that "No man hath seen
God at any time; the only begotten Son, which is in
the bosom of the Father, He hath declared Him;"
the conclusion has been drawn, that since no man
hath seen God at any time, when God was seen in the
former dispensation face to face, it must have been by
the Second Person of the Trinity, the Person of the
Son. Oh, you say, it was Christ, it was the Son Who
was seen. Let us see what this leads to. No less
than the denial of the proper deity of Christ! For if
"No man hath seen God at any time," and yet the
Son was seen throughout the ages, then the Son could
not be God; for, if He had been God, He could not
have been seen.

No, it was the Manifestation of the Triune God by
Angelic ministration, when God was seen.

As an illustration, refer to Isaiah vi. 1. "In the year that King Uzziah died, I saw also the Lord." (*Heb.* Adonahy).

Mark, it is not the title Jehovah, but Adonahy, the *plural* of Adohn that is used; a title expressing the sovereignty of God. Isaiah saw the Triune God "upon a throne, high and lifted up." These things said Isaiah when he saw the glory of Christ, and "spake of Him." (John xii. 41). Where and how did he see the glory of the Son? Not alone, not according to the idea of Arianism, or the theory that it was the Son only; but he saw Him in the glory of the Godhead.

Now observe, in harmony with this, the Seraphim cried one to another, "Holy, holy, holy is Jehovah of Hosts." Then again in verse 8, we read "I heard the voice of Adonahy"—the Sovereign, Triune God—asking, "Whom shall I send?" God in His unity—"And who will go for Us?"—God, the Triune God. This is very important to be understood.

By the title *El*, the oneness of God is expressed, as the One Great Originator, the Great First Cause of all

Eloah, still in the singular, like the last, is expressive of Him, as the one Supreme Object of Worship.

Elohim, is a plural word, which occurs very frequently in the Old Testament Scriptures, and which is expressive of Trinity in Unity.

Again, for the title LORD we have three words in the Hebrew. First, *Adohn* in the singular number, which is used of Christ in Psalm cx. "Jehovah said unto my Lord"—*(Adohn).* And in verse 5 of the same Psalm, there is another title used—*Adonahy.*

In the title JEHOVAH we see how the largeness, the infinitude of the Divine Mind is brought down to human capacity. Let us take that word and examine it—JEHOVAH. Everlastingness is expressed in this title—past, present, and future. He which is, He which was, and He that is to come. These three periods of eternity are here expressed, *Yehi*—"He will be;" *Hove*—"being;" and *Hayah*—"He was."

Now see, how in the Greek, this title is preserved in all its fulness, and yet at the same time is brought down to the human mind. In Rev. i. 4 and 5, we see that Jehovah is expressed in the Greek as Him "which is, which was, and which is to come." Mark the perfection of the expression—

"FROM HIM WHICH IS."

This is not in the present tense in the Greek, as we might suppose from the English, but the present participle, and expresses continuous being,—He always is, the ever-existing One. Thus, " He which is " corresponds to the centre syllable of the word Jehovah, which is also the present participle " *Hove* "— being, implying "which still is."

" WHICH WAS " is not in the Greek, the aorist, or past tense ; but in the *imperfect*, which expresses continuance in the past, He Who ever is, is the One Who ever was, corresponding with the last syllable of Jehovah, " *Hayab*,"—He was.

" WHICH IS TO COME." This is not as you might suppose the future tense, but it is the *present participle* again, and expresses that He always is the coming One, He is ever to come, and corresponds with the first syllable of the title Jehovah— *Yehi*, "which is " the long and continuous tense, " He will be."

The title Jehovah, occurs more than 7000 times in the Old Testament, though only rendered Jehovah in

the Authorized Version 7 times. It is confounded
with other titles. For example, for the 7000 times it
occurs in the Original, it is translated about 800 times
by the word "God."

JAH or YAH is the grandest title by which God
has been pleased to reveal Himself to man, and
expresses Him as the essentially Eternal One, to
Whom past, present, and future is one Eternal *now*.
The *Eternity* of God is expressed in the title Jah, and
everlastingness in that of Jehovah.

Well may we exclaim in the language of Dr. Watts.

> "Great God, how infinite are Thou !
> What worthless worms are we !
> Let the whole race of creatures bow,
> And pay their praise to Thee.
> Thy throne eternal ages stood,
> Ere seas and stars were made :
> Thou art the Ever-living God,
> Were all the nations dead."

Better still, is this expressed in the Scripture, "Extol
Him that rideth upon the Heavens by His name JAH,
and rejoice before Him (Psalms lxviii. 4). The
Hebrew word rendered "Heavens" is not the usual word

employed by the Holy Spirit to express heavens (as in Gen. i. 1), but it is "*Harahboth*," which implies desolateness, or a vast unformed void, or the infinitudes of the universe.   Space is infinite, while creation and the universe, however vast, are limited.   God is infinite ; to His existence there is no limit.

God is ever-present in this vast unformed void, that angels' wings may never reach nor angels' ken penetrate.

"Extol Him who rideth on the vast infinitudes of space by His name JAH ; and rejoice before Him." He is as infinite in His glory, as He is infinite in His being, in His power, and in His existence.   By this name JAH He who fills the infinitudes of eternity and space, let Him be praised.

Now I want you to observe, that this is the reason why the Hebrew has, strictly speaking, only two tenses, the long and the short, though we have the three periods, past, present, and future, otherwise expressed.   The reason for this is, it is taking God's view of the matter, to Whom past, present, and future is one eternal present.   God inhabits eternity, all is present to Him.   We inhabit but a minute.   A minute is composed of 60 seconds, and we are but carried from the one to another.

Suppose, in building a room, the architect designs that so many persons shall be accommodated. Well, he allows so many inches for each individual, reckoning that each individual will occupy that portion of the room. Now, suppose a very minute insect, so small as scarcely to be observed by the human eye unless aided by a powerful microscope—suppose that minute insect passes across that portion of the room allotted to one individual, it will appear to it to be a great space, while to a human being it appears but a step. This is a simple illustration of how our measure of time, must appear, in the eye of Him Who fills infinitude, and Who is Ever-existing.

Now, the stroke of the clock, is the knell of a departed hour ; but hereafter, we shall have an eternity to spend over the precious discoveries of Himself, God has made in His word. What we need at present is the teaching of that Holy Spirit, Who searcheth all things, even the deep things of God. Not only is the word of God a telescope to reveal to us the largeness of the Divine Mind, the glories of heaven, and of the world to come, it is also a microscope, by which we discover the minute perfections which abound on every page. For while God is great in great things, He is very great in little things.

Creation and Reconstruction.

"IN the beginning God created the heaven (the heavens) and the earth." (Gen. i. 1-3). Thus opens the record of Divine truth given in the Sacred Scriptures. God gives us an insight into the beginnings of things. There was a period in the vast expanse of eternity when God, Father, Son, and Spirit existed alone. He is the first and the last. That eternity of Divine existence had no beginning, and can have no end, He is eternal and unchanging. It is not here the beginning of the Son of God, for He was co-eternal with the Father and the Spirit, nor is it here the beginning of the Holy Ghost, He is "The Eternal Spirit." The eternal Father was never childless, the eternal Son never an orphan, the eternal Spirit was ever with the Father and the Son.

But here we are introduced into the beginning of

creation ; the period when created things came into existence: when out of nothing, God created the heavens and the earth : this is revealed for faith.

Philosophers vainly seek to trace back the origin of things to a protoplasm, and thence to evolve all manner of existence. God "taketh the wise in their own craftiness." "By faith we understand that the worlds were framed by the word of God, so that things which are seen, were not made of things which do appear." (Heb. xi. 3). Matter is not eternal. Out of nothing the material universe was brought into existence, by the power of God. Faith sees that everything has its origin in the omnipotence and omniscience of a God of boundless love. The title for "God" here is in the plural, Elohim, the eternally Three in One, the Three Persons in the adorable Godhead, who united not only in the formation of man as seen in verse 26, "Let us make man in our image," but also, in the beginning; Father, Son, and Spirit, by one act of creative power, by the creative word of His might, and by the volition of the creating Spirit, brought out of nothing, the universe into being. The verb "created" is in the singular, expressive of Trinity acting in Unity. "Whatsoever God doeth, it shall be for ever." (Eccles. iii. 14).

That which is once brought into being, material or spiritual, is for ever; there is no such word as annihilation in Scripture—that is an invention of man. This world in the last great day, will melt with fervent heat, but every element is indestructible.

The new heavens and the new earth will be made out of the materials of the first. An atom brought into existence would require omnipotence to put it out of being. Do not listen to those who tell you there is no such thing as "the fire that never shall be quenched," that there is no endless torment; in the necessity of things it cannot be otherwise. What is, shall ever be. Oh, the solemnity of existence! To be, is to be for ever, eternally happy, or eternally cursed. May the Spirit of God bring home to all hearts the question, "Who among us shall dwell with the devouring fire? Who among us shall dwell with everlasting burnings?" (Isa. xxxiii. 14.)

We think of heaven so vaguely. Here is meant the material, starry heavens, as in Psa. viii. 3.: "When I consider Thy heavens."

Or, as the poet sings :—

How beauteous ! How wondrous ! Fain, fain would I see
Your secrets unrobed of their mystery,
Fain would I cleave the dark dome of the night,
Soaring up like a thought to your islands of light.
Fain would I ravish your secrets Divine,
By what forms ye are peopled, and wherefore ye shine ;
By what laws ye are governed, and formed on what plan,
I would know, but I may not ; this is not for man.
Great, glorious, the day when the Author of all,
Having spake ye from nought, and ye rose at His call.
Through the regions of space from His hand ye were hurled,
Dark myriads of atoms, each atom a world.
While each sped to its point in the boundless expanse,
And ye caught your first light from the light of His glance,
His power in one moment fixed each in its spot—
One moment remitted, ye sink, and are not.
What a dot is this earth 'mid ye orbs of the sky !
And, compared with this earth, what an atom am I !
Yet I, with my mind's cobweb plummet, would sound
That Mind which hath known nor creation nor bound !
Would fathom the depths of His wondrous decree !
Can a fly grasp a world ? a shell compass the sea ?
No ; this to weak man is allowed, and no more—
He may wonder, and worship, admire, and adore.

Those starry orbs and this firm and massive earth

sprang in the beginning into existence at the fiat of the
Triune God.   "He spake, and it was done ; He commanded, and it hath stood fast."   Psa. xxxiii. 9.   " By
His Spirit He garnished the Heavens."   Job xxvi. 13.
How did He create them?   All His works bear the
impress "very good."   Gen. i. 31.   The Heavens
were created pure, the earth was created not "in vain,"
literally, "not void."   Isaiah xlv. 18.   This we are
expressly told.

We should separate the first verse from the rest of
the chapter, as it speaks only of the beginning of
things by the creative power of a Triune God.   What
interval of time there was between the first and
second verses it is impossible to estimate.

Verse 2 : "And the earth was without form, and
void ; and darkness was upon the face of the deep."
The second verse begins not with creation, but with
re-construction,—a re-making of things already in
existence.   Notice the two words "create" and
"make" in this chapter.

In Ex. xx., verse 11, we read : "In six days Jehovah
made (not created) the heavens and the earth;" made,
that is, constructed them out of existing materials.

The materials were there, but by what catastrophe they became " without form and void " we know not.

The history of this world commences with verse 2, B.C. 4004. Previous to this, Angels had fallen, for in chapter iii. Satan comes as a seducing, lying spirit, on the scene. He was one of the Angels who kept not their first estate (Jude 6), a master spirit, Lucifer, son of the morning, " who had said in his heart, I will be like the Most High." (Isa. xiv. 14.) Under his leadership there was a " strike," and those associated with him fell, and are " reserved in everlasting chains, under darkness unto the judgment of the great day." (Jude 6.)

In eternity, what we know not now will be fully revealed ; but the fact remains, that when the history of this world commenced, there was chaos and confusion : the earth answered not its original purpose and design.

It was in its second stage of being, a mass of matter, shapeless and unprofitable, no longer showing forth the glory of God. We have here a type or shadow, of man's first upright condition by creation, and of his present state through the fall. Man was formed in the image of His Maker, with a capacity to

glorify Him.   God created him upright, holy,
righteous ; of the dust of the earth was he built up ;
and the Spirit of Elohim breathed into him the breath
of life.   Man is a triune being.   The Devil, or Satan,
in the guise of a serpent, the most subtle of the
creatures tempted, and man fell.

" Man, in the image of his Maker formed," became
" Man in the image of his tempter fallen."   No longer
fit for the society of God, and intimacy with God, nor
for fellowship with one another without shame ; hence
they made their fig-leaf covering, and went out of the
presence of God, hiding, when in the cool of the day
God was wont to walk with them.   Death in the soul
had commenced, the body had become mortal, and
the second, the eternal death was only averted by
faith in the promise of the woman's Seed.   This is
man's condition now.   Men say he is noble, and has
stupendous powers.

Just as the earth, when without form and void, had
in it its original elements ; so man, though fallen, still
retains the lofty intellect, penetrating eye, and skilful
hand ; but no longer is he fit for communion with
God, nor for the inheritance of the saints in light.

If unconverted, would he wish to go to heaven to-day, if he might, just as he is? The moment he grasps the idea of what God is, in His purity, of what heaven is, he would say, " No, hide me from the face of Him who sits upon the throne." Man might be of incalculable benefit to his fellows, but is he?

Look at Napoleon the Great ! What was he as a benefactor to the race? He looked on men as food for powder, in order to carry out his ambitious designs. If it suits man's purpose to do others good, he will.

The lowest type of man is when religion is made the cloak of hypocrisy, saying, "Stand by, I am holier than thou."

Darkness covers the earth, and gross darkness the people. Is there not a plague as of Egyptian darkness creeping over colleges, pulpits, and pews? Look at the heathen and Mahommedan parts of the world, at the superstition of Romanism and Ritualism, with its "dim religious light," as they glory to call it. "Darkness is on the face of the deep." "If any among you seemeth to be wise in this world, let him become a fool, that he may be wise ; for the wisdom of this world is foolishness with God. For it is

written, "He taketh the wise in their own craftiness."
And again, "Jehovah knoweth the thoughts (or
reasonings), of the wise, that they are vain" (1 Cor.
iii. 18-20). Are your souls in darkness? or, is your
pathway that of the just which shineth more and more
unto the perfect day?

Verse 2: "And the Spirit of God moved (was
fluttering), upon the face of the waters." Blessed be
God, this is also true of the present time. Man has
fallen, is in darkness, but the Spirit of the Triune God
is hovering over him.

The Holy Ghost has come, the Comforter has
descended from the throne of the Father and the Son,
to convict man of sin. There is no greater blessing
in this dark, chaotic condition of man, than that the
Holy Spirit convicts of these three things: of the
presence of sin, of a want of righteousness, and of a
judgment to come (John xvi. 8-11). When a lost
sinner is awakened, the work of the Spirit of God is
unmistakeable, in conviction of sin, and in showing
that he needs the washing of regeneration, and the
renewing of the Holy Ghost; that he needs to be born
again, formed anew, re-created.

Verse 3 : And God said, "let there be light," and there was light. To this the apostle refers in 2 Cor. iv. 6—"God, who commanded the light to shine out of darkness, hath shined in our hearts, to give the light of the knowledge of the glory of God in the face of Jesus Christ."

The same Divine Eternal Spirit who convicts man of his unprofitableness, and blindness, also reveals God's remedy in the Person and work of His beloved Son.

By the Word of God received into the heart by faith, which is God's testimony to Christ, in the power of the Holy Ghost, there is regeneration, a new creation ; old things pass away, behold all things become new ; and all things are of God.

The Fall.

GENESIS III.

THE creation and fall of man lie at the very foundation of revealed truth. Materialists deny the first, and Rationalists the latter. It is well in these days to be strong as to these fundamental truths.

As the Lord Jesus said " If any will do His will, he shall know of the doctrine whether it be of God." If we are willing to hear and obey, God will speak with majesty and power. When God's Word is brought home to the inward consciousness by the Spirit of God, there is no doubt of the majesty and truth of that Word ; " God who commanded the light to shine out of darkness, hath shined into our hearts, to give the light of the knowledge of the glory of God in the face of

Jesus Christ." He will leave no part dark, so far as the light penetrates all is clear, certain, sure. The secret of faith in God, is receiving God's Word like the Thessalonians of old, not as the word of man, but as it is in truth, the Word of God, which worketh effectually in them that believe. For "faith cometh by hearing, and hearing by the Word of God."

If we begin with God, "then shall we know, if we follow on to know the Lord;" and thus we shall grow in grace.

If we begin with reason and human opinions, and doubts, Satan will becloud the mind, and put a veil before our face, so that God's revelation will be shut out: this is the secret of unbelief, both as to the veracity of God's Word, and of the Gospel of His grace, (2 Cor. iv. 3, 4).

If we begin to doubt the truth of Scripture, as to the fall of man, the Deity of Christ, the Personality of the Holy Ghost, and eternal judgment, the foundations of the soul will be undermined, and every other form of false doctrine may speedily follow.

If the Scripture is not truly the Word of God there can be no regeneration, for we are said to be "born again by the Word of God which liveth and abideth for ever" (1 Peter i. 23). And it is the Holy Spirit of God by His Divine power, Who through the Word regenerates the sinner.

Genesis iii. 1 states the fact, that "the serpent was more subtil than any beast of the field." Satan who is mighty in intellect and skill, having examined the animal creation, discovered in the serpent an agent most suited to effect his design. Then as a skilful general, he searches for a weak point in the citadel of Mansoul. Why did he not assault Adam first? If he had, in all probability he would have failed; his first arrow would not have hit. Had he put the question to Adam, "Yea, hath God said? Adam might at once have replied, "Who are you to suggest a doubt as to the veracity of God's Word?" Yes, God hath said, "I heard him."

So far as is recorded, Eve had not heard God say this. It was before her formation, that Adam had received the command and prohibition; and thus Eve received it at second-hand. The truth which we receive from God Himself, remains fixed and established in the mind; but that which we receive at second-hand, is open to the assaults of Satan. Satan began by suggesting a doubt as to whether God had spoken at all, " Yea, hath God said." And is He not repeating His tactics at the present day, by raising the enquiry, " Is there any divinely-inspired Word of God ? Is there any infallible guide to certainty and truth? Was the Pentateuch written by Moses ? Can we receive every word, as written under the direct superintendence of the Holy Ghost ? When Satan cannot altogether set aside the Word of God, he attempts to pervert it. Thus in his question to Eve he puts the prohibition first, and leaves out the gracious permission altogether.

By this means suggesting an erroneous view of the character of God, as though He would withhold any real good.

The woman answers nobly ; she replies first to his insinuation. " We may eat of the fruit of the trees of the garden ;" a beautiful example of repelling the assault of Satan by quoting the words of God to her husband; (see chapter ii. 16), even as Christ did, when tempted by the Devil in the wilderness. Whether God had said to Adam " Neither shall ye touch it," we are not informed.

But we must beware when controverting error, that we do not add to the words of God. When, however, instead of quoting the express declaration, "In the day thou eatest thereof thou shalt surely die," Eve toned it down into the uncertain form of "Lest ye die." She gave an opportunity to the enemy, of which he was not slow to take advantage. In like manner if we admit the possibility of "A Larger Hope," we lay ourselves open to temptation. We are only safe, when we abide by the exact language of Scripture. God put man into Paradise, and gave him ample room for enjoyment; but placed him under one restriction, to show him that even there, he was to be a man under authority. Satan now advanced a step further, by bringing in his own lie,—"Ye shall not surely die," in direct denial of God's Word. Man became a living soul by the inbreathing of Divine life, by a Triune God.

So long as he continued in communion with Him, his soul lived; but when this communion with the Holy Ghost was broken by his disobedience, his soul died. From that moment, his body became mortal, and he was only rescued from the second, or spiritual and eternal death, through faith in God's promise of the woman's Seed. "By one man sin entered into the world and death by sin." But when our first parents had believed God's promise, God immediately brought in the foreshadowing type of redemption. Before God could clothe Adam and Eve in coats of skin, an animal must have been sacrificed, the innocent died for the guilty ; and the first blood shed on the earth was that of expiation.

Satan having given God the lie, brought in a revelation of his own, and professedly on the authority of God : "For God doth know that in the day ye eat thereof, then your eyes shall be opened, and ye shall be as gods, knowing good and evil."

There was truth in what Satan said, for in the day when they had eaten of the fruit of that tree, then their eyes were opened, but it was to the discovery of their own nakedness and shame. And from thenceforth they obtained a knowledge of good and evil which they had not before, but it was a knowledge of good forfeited, and evil secured. Instead, however, of becoming more like God, much of the glory of God in which they had been created was lost ; and man became more and more conformed to the pattern of his tempter.

"And Adam called his wife's name Eve, because she was the mother of all living. Unto Adam and his wife did Jehovah God, make coats of skin, and clothed them." (Not skins, it was the skin of one victim in which both were clothed) Verse 20, 21.

Our first parents beguiled by the old serpent the devil, had been deceived into disbelief and disobedience of God's Word, afterwards, having been called into God's presence, were there convicted of sin and confessed it.

In the sentence pronounced on the serpent, and on the enemy who had used him for an agent, they had heard the glad tidings of redemption. God had said "I will put enmity between thee and the woman, and between thy seed and her Seed ; it (or He), shall bruise thy head, and thou shall bruise His heel" (verse 15). This is the first promise and prophecy, and contains within itself the seed-germ, and embryo of all the promises and prophecies.

Wrapped up in these simple words, is the mystery of God, and the mystery of Christ, "in Whom are hid all treasures of wisdom and knowledge" (Col. ii. 3), just as in an acorn, the future oak and forest is contained. In the bruising of the heel of the woman's Seed was taught the cross, and redemption through the Saviour's atoning death. And in the bruising of the serpent's head, was foretold the Saviour's victory over him who hath the power of death; and the prospect of the resurrection from the dead.

Our first parents believed the announcement of God concerning His beloved Son, which was accompanied by the power of the Holy Ghost. Adam had just heard the solemn word concerning the death of the body, from the lips of God,—"In the sweat of thy face shalt thou eat bread, until thou return unto the ground; for out of it wast thou taken : for dust thou art, and unto dust shalt thou return " (verse 19).

Adam had the sentence of death in himself that he should not trust in himself, but in God Who raiseth the dead ; and under the teaching of the Holy Spirit, in the prediction of the woman's Seed, his faith laid hold of the promise of eternal life. And though through their sin, death had entered into the world, and henceforth would pass to all men; instead of calling his wife by a name signifying death, he called her "the mother of all living," for Eve signifies " Living." This was the confession of his faith; "for with the heart man believeth unto righteousness, and with the mouth confession is made unto salvation " (Rom. x. 10).

Eve subsequently confessed the same faith, for she called her first-born son Cain (that is " Acquired "), trusting, that she had acquired the promised Seed, the Man Jehovah. In this she was mistaken as she afterwards discovered; hence she called her second son Abel (that is "Vanity").

God had said to Adam, "In the day that thou eatest (of the forbidden fruit) thou shalt surely die ;" and this threatening was fulfilled : for, through their act of disobedience, the communion of our first parents with God was broken. And as life in the body can only be maintained by breathing the atmospheric air ; so life in the soul can only be sustained by communion with God, through the Holy Ghost, and this only can be regained and continued, by faith in God's Word.

The first animal death which occured in Paradise was that of an innocent victim, the substitution of the guiltless for the guilty, the first blood shed was typically the blood of atonement, expiation and redemption.

All future Patriarchial and Levitical foreshadowing sacrifices, were embodied in this first offering, hence we must apply the principles afterwards developed, to this first sacrifice. The Levitical law, required that the one who brought the sacrifice, for sin, or for acceptance, was to kill the victim. Before the Aaronic order of the priesthood was instituted, the patriarch acted as priest. And as on the Day of Atonement, the High Priest presented the blood for himself and his house, so Adam was required to slay the victim, and present the blood for himself and his wife. And as the skin of the burnt-offering was apportioned to the priest that offered it, so with the skin of the first victim, God Himself clothed Adam and Eve. The first garment manufactured by man, was the fig-leaved covering, which was as nothing in the sight of God. In the parable in Luke xv., the father commanded the SERVANTS to bring forth the

best robe and put it on the prodigal son; but here there
is no waiting for servants; Jehovah God Himself
clothed them.   God Himself was the first to institute
the foreshadowing sacrifices ; and by clothing our
first parents, He set forth the truth of acceptance in
God's Beloved, and of completeness in Him.

The Spirits Tried.

1 JOHN IV. 1-6.

———

V. 1. "BELOVED, believe not every spirit, but try the spirits whether they are of God; because many false prophets are gone out into the world."

V. 2: Hereby know ye the Spirit of God : every spirit that confesseth that Jesus Christ is come in the flesh is of God.

V. 3: And every spirit that confesseth not that Jesus Christ is come in the flesh, is not of God : and this is that spirit of antichrist, whereof ye have heard that it should come ; and even now already is it in the world.

V. 4: Ye are of God, little children, and have overcome them : because greater is He that is in you than he that is in the world.

V. 5 : They are of the world; therefore speak they of the world, and the world heareth them.

V. 6: We are of God: he that knoweth God heareth us : he that is not of God heareth not us. Hereby know we the spirit of truth, and the spirit of error."

Again and again the Spirit of God has warned us that in the last days perilous times should come; surely now it is so, and false teachers are amongst us. This is truth and warning for the times, a Scripture portion for the day, "because many false prophets are gone out into the world." There may be supernatural power and spiritual energy. We are not to come hastily to the conclusion that every spirit is "of God," though speaking as with the tongues of men and of angels. Not only are arguments to be tried, doctrines and evidences to be weighed, but, above all, the "spirits" are to be tried. What is the spirit which actuates the speaker or the writer? From whence comes this inspiration, this wisdom, this spiritual activity and energy, this marvellous success? Is it of God? Can it be traced up to the Father of spirits, to the Father of lights? Or to another and opposite source? It is most important to discern the source, the secret of the apparent wisdom and success. Reasoning powers, argumentative skill, the flowers of eloquence and oratory are weapons Satan can use. If we enter into conflict with the "spirit of the power of the air" in argument, we shall be beaten. Satan is more dexterous in the use of those weapons than we, the weapons of our warfare are not carnal but spiritual. It is with spiritual weapons we must meet the " doctrines of devils."

The title recently announced for a sermon was " Inspiration measured by our capacity." That is like testing the powers of a telescope by the capacity of human vision. It is like a person going to one of the stupendous telescopes of the day, saying, "I will believe nothing that I cannot see with my own eyes without a telescope." This is exactly the ground we take, if we attempt to test inspiration by our reason. There is an inspiration from beneath, subtle and marvellous ; it is to be tested by the Word of God, by the Spirit of God, and in the sunshine of the presence of God.

" Beloved," this is the language of earnest entreaty and brotherly love.

In the time of our Lord there were three things against which He warned His disciples : the leaven of the Pharisees, which is self-righteousness and ritualism ; the leaven of the Sadduceees, scepticism and the denial of the supernatural ; and the leaven of Herod, a pandering to the spirit of the times.

At the present time there are three sources of error we are warned against. First, THE SPIRIT WHICH IS "NOT OF GOD" (v. 3). Second, THE "SPIRIT OF ANTICHRIST" (v. 3). Third, "THE SPIRIT OF ERROR" (v. 6). How are they to be tested ? Not merely by human faculties, nor by the opinions of others. We should not meet Goliath with Saul's armour. But test the doctrine in the presence of God, by the person of Christ, and by the Word and teaching of the Holy Ghost, with direct application to the Spirit of God.

In verse 2 the words "that" and "is" are not in the original, it is better read, " confesseth Jesus Christ come in the flesh." It is not so much the doctrine as the person, confessing Him. Mark the titles " Jesus," Jehovah the Saviour, a title combining His divinity with His office. It is not simply Oshua,—"salvation," but Jehoshua,—"the salvation of Jehovah." The title

"Christ" means, "The anointed One of Jehovah," conceived, born, anointed, filled with the Holy Ghost, "The Christ" concerning whom God could say to John the Baptist, "Upon whom thou shalt see the Spirit descending, and remaining on Him, the same is He which baptiseth with the Holy Ghost" (John i. 33); who said of Himself in the synagogue of Nazareth, "The Spirit of Jehovah is upon Me, because He hath anointed Me," &c. (Luke iv. 18, 19). He was the Antitype of the "fine flour" unleavened, but mingled with oil (Lev. ii.), saturated with oil, no feeling, thought, desire, teaching, merely human, but pervaded with the Spirit; hence He was often misunderstood. When He spoke of water and the new birth in John iii., He referred to "the washing of regeneration and renewing of the Holy Ghost." When speaking of the bread from heaven, it was in reference to Himself, the gift of God to a perishing world.

"Come in the flesh." The Gnostic error said Christ was a phantom. We have also to mark His pre-existence, "I came forth from the Father, and am come into the world" (John xvi. 28). He was God manifest in flesh (1 Tim. iii. 16). There is none other name given among men whereby we can be saved.   Those who will not own His deity, pre-existence, and eternal Sonship, and that He is the Anointed, the Messiah of the Old Testament, and the Christ of the New, are "not of God."   That spirit that confesses, magnifies, and maintains these truths "is of God."   This involves the recognition of Jesus Christ as a Divine Person, and that the eternal Spirit is co-existent, and of equal glory with the Father and the Son.   The personality of the Holy Ghost must be acknowledged, for if there is no anointing Spirit, there is no anointed Messiah.   If there be no inspiring Spirit, there can be no inspired Word, and no Word of God on which implicit confidence can be placed.

Verse 4 : " Ye are of God, little children, and have overcome them."   Why ?   Because you have superior reasoning powers ?   No.   But because " greater is He that is in you than he that is in the world."   " Ye have an unction from the Holy One " (1 John ii. 20-27), and He keeps you steadfast.   The secret of overcoming is dependence on the Holy Ghost.

There are three characteristics of false doctrine which have specially to be tested in these last days, namely, the spirit which is "not of God," but opposed to the truth and honour of God the Father. This is manifested in Atheism, Deism, Agnosticism, Rationalism, and so forth. Second, the "the spirit of antichrist" as opposed to the glory and truth of the Son of God, denying His Divinity, eternal Sonship, vicarious sufferings, and glorious offices. This is manifested in Arianism, Socinianism, and the "downgrade" doctrines of the present day. Third, "the spirit of error," which, while admitting the Scriptures to be the basis of doctrine and faith, pervert them, misinterpreting and misapplying the words of truth This spirit is opposed to the Spirit of Truth, the Holy Ghost, the Inspirer of the sacred Word, and the only unction from the Holy One by which that Word can be understood.

The working of this spirit may be traced in Christadelphianism, Mormonism, and various other forms of doctrinal error. Mark, to discern the spirit of truth we must be "of God." Shall I go to one who does not know God for instruction about Him? For a man to teach theology he must know God, be born of God, be filled and taught by the Spirit of

God. Every word of God is pure and precious. "Thus saith Jehovah," stamps the Word of God with authority, importance, and power. If men say there is no Word of God, no wonder if the Bible be a dead letter to them. "If any man will do His will, he shall know of the doctrine whether it be of God" (John vii. 17.) If the confession which is made with the lip be the result of Divine revelation, as with Peter when he said, "Thou art the Christ, the Son of the living God" Matt. xvi. 16, 17), on such a confession the blessing of God can rest.

True Wisdom and Strength.

1 Cor. i. 27-31.

V. 27-29. "GOD hath chosen the foolish things of the world to confound the wise; and God hath chosen the weak things of the world to confound the things that are mighty; and base things of the world, and things which are despised, hath God chosen, yea, and things which are not, to bring to nought things that are: that no flesh should glory in His presence." This is the purpose of our God, "to stain the pride of all glory, and to bring into contempt all the honourable of the earth" (Isa. xxiii. 9). As He said by the prophet, "Let not the wise man glory in his wisdom, neither let the mighty man glory in his might, let not the rich man glory in his riches: but let him that glorieth, glory

in this, that he understandeth and knoweth Me, that I
am Jehovah which exercise lovingkindness, judgment
and righteousness in the earth" (Jer. ix. 23, 24).
Verily, if we come into the presence of our God, we
realize that "the grass withereth, the flower fadeth,
because the Spirit of Jehovah bloweth upon it ; surely
the people is grass " (Isa. xl. 7).

> The more His glories strike the eye,
> The humbler we shall lie.

It is vain to glory in the presence of the God of the
whole earth, but the believer can glory in his God,
can rejoice in Christ Jesus, with joy unspeakable and
full of glory ; for we are complete in Him who is the
head of all principality and power (Col. ii. 9-10). It
is for the believer to glory in Christ Jesus, who of God
is made unto us wisdom, and righteousness, and
sanctification, and redemption, so that we are complete
in Him in whom dwells all the fullness of the Godhead
bodily.   " But we have this treasure in earthen vessels,
that the excellency of the power may be of God, and
not of us " (2 Cor. iv. 7).   We have it not in ourselves,
but in Christ Jesus.   We do not read God made us
wise, righteous, holy, with the power to redeem our-

selves ; that would be to exalt the creature.   Then we should have somewhat wherein to glory, and might go about saying that we were perfect.

But mark, GOD made Him all this to us.   " Of Him are we in Christ Jesus, who of God is made unto us us wisdom."   God Himself, it is all of God the Father, for "every good gift and every perfect gift cometh down from the Father of lights" (James i. 17). He hath treasured up all our treasures in the person of His Son.   We want to realise that all the stores of wisdom and grace are in Christ, who is the wisdom and power of God (1 Cor. i. 24).   He is Jehovah-Tzidkenu, in Christ Jesus, for our righteousness is in Him, and He is made righteousness to us.   Christ also has sanctified Himself that we may be sanctified through the truth (John xvii. 19).   In Him we have the fulness of the Spirit according to the riches of grace Divine.   We do not boast in ourselves, but we rejoice in Christ Jesus, as the true circumcision who have no confidence in the flesh (Phil. iii. 3).   How is Christ made all this to us practically?   How is He made to us individually wisdom ?   The mere knowledge that God made Christ all this to us will not

are we made complete in Him? The answer is plain.
Just as Christ was about to ascend to His God and
our God, He said, "I will send the Comforter."
"Tarry till endued with power from on high." The
Holy Spirit was to take of the things of Jesus and
reveal them (John xiv., xv., xvi). It is by the Holy
Ghost that we are made all this in Christ.

WISDOM is treasured up in Christ Jesus, but we have
the unction from the Holy One, that we might know all
things, so as to need no human teacher. The treasures
of wisdom and knowledge hid in Christ Jesus, the Spirit
communicates while we are dependent on Him, and
taught by Him; thus we "have the mind of Christ."

How is Christ practically RIGHTEOUSNESS to the
believer? It is when walking "not after the flesh, but
after the Spirit" (Rom. viii. 1-4). We are "created
in Christ Jesus unto good works" (Eph. ii. 10), and
living in the power of the Spirit of God, the fruits of
the Spirit are brought forth (Gal. v. 22, 23).

SANCTIFICATION. "Through sanctification of the
Spirit" (2 Thess. ii. 13). It is He who spiritually
sanctifies.

REDEMPTION. It is by the Spirit we are sealed unto the day of full redemption (Eph. iv. 30). He gives the joy of redemption now ; He is the earnest of the purchased possession till we receive the redemption of the body (Eph. i. 14), redemption from every woe to the full possession of joy. The Spirit takes of the things of Christ and reveals them to us, giving grace and power to live. Sanctification is holy living, practical righteousness, living and walking in the presence of God. We live and abide in Christ, as we are strengthened with might by His Spirit in the inner man, Christ dwelling in our hearts by faith (Eph. iii. 16, 17) ; thus we receive out of the fulness of God. We are too apt to confide in isolated doctrines ; we want to live in the fulness of Divine truth, to live in the presence of God who has given us all in Christ, living, not we, but Christ in us. There must be the third link, the unbroken fellowship of the Holy Ghost; He sheds abroad the love of God so that we may bring forth the fruits of the Spirit which are by Jesus Christ to the glory and praise of God. Thus the secret of holy living may be summed up in these three things—walking in the presence of God ; abiding in

Christ; and living and walking in the unbroken fellowship of the Holy Ghost.